MAT CUTTING
&
DECORATION

COLUMBA PUBLISHING COMPANY, INC.

AKRON, OHIO

LIBRARY OF PROFESSIONAL PICTURE FRAMING
Volume Two
MAT CUTTING & DECORATION
by Vivian Carli Kistler, MCPF, GCF, Adv.

Revised Edition 2009
Published by Columba Publishing Co. Inc.
Akron, Ohio USA
Copyright 1987, 1998, 2001, 2003, 2009
All international rights reserved
Manufactured in the United States of America
ISBN 0-938655-01-9

Editors:
    Vivian Carli Kistler
    Sheri L. Galat
PrePress:
    Carli Kistler Miller
Illustrations:
    Marla Strasburg Crawford
    Vivian Kistler
Photography:
    Andy Fiala,
    Heather Protz
    Barbara Schlueter

20 19 18 17 16 15 14 13 12

Please request permission or further information from the Permissions Department
Columba Publishing Co. Inc.
154 Pembroke Rd, Akron, OH 44333
Telephone: 330.836.2619 Fax: 330.836.9659
www.columbapublishing.com

ACKNOWLEDGMENTS

Aleen's Tacky Glue
Artgum Eraser
Crescent Cardboard Co. LLC
    Rag Mat
    Classic Museum Solid Rag Mat
    Perfect Mount Film
H.F. Esterly
    Speed-Mat
The Fletcher-Terry Co.
    Glass & board wall-mounted cutter
    Mat cutter
3M
    810 permanent tape
    811 removable tape
    ATG double-stick tape
KeenCut
    Glass & board wall-mounted cutter
    Straight-line mat cutter
Elmer's Bienfang
    Fusion 4000
    ColorMount
    Mighty Core
    X-Acto Knife
Lineco, Inc.
    Tapes & Adhesives
Logan Graphic Products, Inc.
    Mat cutters
Yes Paste
Sobo Glue

MAT CUTTING
&
DECORATION

VOLUME 2

OF THE

LIBRARY OF PROFESSIONAL PICTURE FRAMING

BY

VIVIAN C. KISTLER, MCPF, GCF

COLUMBA PUBLISHING COMPANY, INC.

AKRON, OHIO, USA

Special Thanks

to the following picture framers and industry leaders who have contributed directly and indirectly to this book. By sharing their ideas and techniques, they have added to the professionalism of the picture framing industry.

John Alley

Carolyn Birchenall, CPF

Bill Bradley, MCPF

Pat Bradley, MCPF

Brian Buell

Charles Carithers

Herb Carithers

Roy Carter, CPF

Jim Cook, CPF

Jean Deemer

Guy Downing, CPF

Kaye Evans, CPF, GCF

Jennifer Eddy, CPF

Jim Eyrich, CPF

Paul Frederick, CPF

Sheri Leigh Galat, CPF

Charles Galazzo, CPF

Don Gottfredson, MCPF

Gene Green

Judy Greek

Carol Halsey

Bob Hendrixson

Sean Hunt, CPF

Martha Hobson

Steve Kocsis, CPF

Betty Kylin, CPF

Larry Lasher

Harry Lewis

Robin Lockwood

M. David Logan

Paul MacFarland, CPF, GCF

Cass Bricker Mayfield, CPF

Robert Mayfield, CPF, GCF

Stoney Newberry, CPF

Dameron Owen, CPF

William Parker, MCPF, GCF

Greg Perkins, CPF

Hugh Phibbs

Nona Powers, CPF, GCF

John Ranes, CPF, GCF

Jo Ann Richardson

Marsha Saum

Nap Smith

Billy Sproles

Mary Julie Thomasson, CPF

Paul Ulichney

Harry Watkins, CPF

Cynthia Westlake

Brian Wolf, CPF, GCF

CONTENTS

The Library of Professional Picture Framing

The six-volume set is designed to provide detailed information on the theory, materials and procedures of professional picture framing.

Volume 1 PICTURE FRAMING

The first volume is a practical reference guide that deals with the basic elements of framing, from the history of period frames to the application of a dust cover and hangers. The purpose of Volume 1 is to give a solid background, providing an overview of framing as both a craft and an art form.

Other volumes in *The Library* examine specific facets of picture framing in depth. These books provide comprehensive coverage of the many techniques available to and practiced by the professional framer.

Volume 2 MAT CUTTING & DECORATION

Step-by-step directions for 50 + mat cuts. Measurements, proportion, color selection, inlay, offsets, v-grooves, color panels, cove mats, fabric wrapped, lattice, multiple opening layouts, Kobe corners, circles, ovals, gothic, fancy corners, 6 & 8 sided, and more! Regular straight-line mat cutters and CMCs.

Volume 3 NEEDLEWORK FRAMING

Block & stretch needlepoint 12 methods of mounting needlework and textiles. Fifteen projects. Cleaning, repairs & pressing. Directions to frame crewel, needlepoint, cross-stitch, antique samplers, quilt, scarf, kimono, carpet, scroll, hanky, doily, Persian art, papyrus, weaving & flag.

Volume 4 CONSERVATION FRAMING

Handling Art on Paper. Choosing glazing. Making hinges & supports for all types of art on paper. Deacidify papers. Encapsulation. Projects include framing watercolors, papyrus, pastels, photos, skin documents. Cleaning and repairs.

Volume 5 MOUNTING METHODS

Dry, Wet, Spray and Pressure-Sensitive mounting methods. Adhesives & boards. Selecting a process. Bubbles & buckling. Equipment. Reversing mounting procedures. Projects include: canvas transfer, puzzles, rubbings, cut-outs, fabric, photos, oversized & plastic items.

Volume 6 FRAMING PHOTOGRAPHY

Photography time line. Identify and frame antique photos. Framing methods for: ambrotype, daguerreotype, albumen, tintype, Ilfochrome Classics®, Polaroid®, snapshots and more! Mounting photos with dry, pressure-sensitive, wet & spray methods. Projects.

Volume 7 FRAMING COLLECTIBLES

Methods to support over 120 different items! Shadow box framing. Dozens of projects provided by 46 framers. Fourteen methods for support and attachment. Building deep frames, double-sided frames, and frames with doors. How to frame: Sports Equipment, Christening Gowns, Musical Instruments, Bark Paintings, Olympic Torches, Seashells, Military Medals, Guns, Animation Cels, Vintage Photographs, Dolls, Jerseys, pucks, & more...

CHAPTER ONE

THE BASICS

Matting (sometimes called "paper mat" or "mount" in Europe) is a border that surrounds the art within a picture frame. Although several materials could be used to make mats, they are usually made of matboard. Except for a small range of boards made from compressed pulp, matboard is composed of several layers, including a cover sheet, center core and a lining paper on the back. The cover sheet carries color and sometimes texture; the core may also be colored.

Matboards are available in hundreds of colors, surface patterns, and finishes. The standard size is 32x40", but 40x60" is available in an increasing range of colors, and a few colors are available even larger, including 4'x8'.

The quality of a matboard depends on the materials and methods used by the manufacturer. Although matboards are designed and manufactured to last for many years, matting (and framing) is not meant to last unchanged forever. It is important for customers to understand that age and environment affect framing just as they affect anything else in a home. A valued piece should be taken to the frame shop every three to five years for inspection and cleaning, allowing problems to be detected and corrected at an early stage.

Matting is an art. Like any art it requires knowledge of materials and methods, and refinement of skills. Not only are proper cutting techniques required, but an understanding of color and proportion of the mat in relationship to the art is very important. Matting provides two significant benefits to framed art—presentation and protection.

PRESENTATION
Picture framing allows the display of artwork and objects in a visually pleasing presentation; matting is often a key element in that presentation. A mat can highlight a color, accent a shape, and of course increase the size of the art. Matboard can be cut, layered, painted and covered to create a fine presentation for any art piece. Matting is used with art on paper (watercolors, posters, newsprint, certificates, photos, etc.)

and sometimes in shadowboxes—but not on oil paintings, acrylic paintings, or other art on canvas. Matting is usually covered by glazing, since the exposed surfaces of all but the fabric-covered boards stay in the best condition when protected. Art on canvas should not be glassed, so fabric-covered wooden liners take the place of matboard to create a presentation border for the art.

PROTECTION
The most important benefit of matting is the protection it provides. The border and its immediate backing provide support for the artwork. Artwork should be attached within the mat unit using methods that allow it to expand and contract with changes in temperature and humidity. The art must be given room to move freely. For example, if it is held down at all four corners, buckling will result in the center because the piece has no other expansion room. Matting also permits air circulation, which allows any moisture that may condense within the frame to dissipate.

Framed items should not be placed directly against the glass, or the result will be buckling, wrinkles, mold formation, and items "sticking" to the glass. Matting provides the support and airspace that prevents these problems. Some customers will insist that a piece be framed without a mat and pressed against the glass—be prepared to explain the potential problems. An alternative to matting is mounting If artwork is mounted for flatness, a spacer should still be used to keep the surface away from the glass.

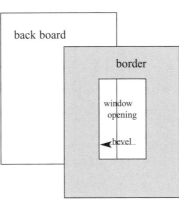

A complete mat consists of a matboard with a window opening and a backing board made from the same type of matboard.

The "decorator" idea of sandwiching a picture between two pieces of glass will also cause wrinkles, and is generally unhealthy for the art. Use a spacer between the glass pieces to allow the art to move with environmental changes, or fully mount the art if it is merely decorative.

Not only are wrinkles and buckles bad for art, they also create dissatisfied customers, and cost the shop time and money spent redoing wrinkled pieces.

Styles of Mats

Museum Style Matting

Typically white, black or pale neutral colors. The art is often placed in the upper area leaving a very large lower margin. Often museums use this style when mounting a collection of different size pieces using frames of uniform size. Especially suitable on small images.

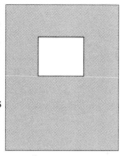

Weighted Bottom Mat

Equal borders on the top and sides, extra width on bottom border. The amount of weight may be slight or moderate, appearing balanced when viewed. Whether rooted in the Victorian tradition of hanging pictures very high on the wall, or in response to a natural visual preference for a solid base, this style is an attractive design option for both traditional and contemporary art.

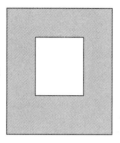

Oriental Style Mat

A traditional oriental proportion based on the proportions of paintings done on scrolls. Used both vertically and horizontally depending on the artwork. To mimic scroll proportions, the narrow sides are one third or less than the width of the wider sides.

Roman/Gothic Mat

This arched design conveys a feeling of tradition, antiquity, and romance. Suitable on Renaissance prints, wedding and ancestral photos. For visual balance, a bit less matting is used on the top than on the sides and bottom. The rounded arch is Roman; the pointed is Gothic.

French Matting

This traditional style, also called wash panels, is created with subtle-colored painted panels and a series of ink lines. Frequently used on 19th century etchings and watercolors, French matting can bring an air of refinement to traditional reproductions as well. For the best visual balance, keep the decorative elements within the first third of mat width from the mat opening.

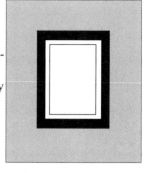

Spandrel Mat

An oval or circle within a rectangle or square is called a spandrel. The curve of a mat opening can give elegance, dignity, and grace to a design. Because oval and circle openings invite central focus, they are especially suited to art which is featured in the center such as vignettes, portraits and sketches.

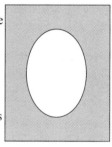

Print Mat

This design is often used to accommodate the size of the artist's printmaking paper. To preserve the value of original art on paper, the paper should not be cut or altered in any way. If the painting, print, drawing, etc. is done on a large sheet of paper, matting can cover the excess "carrier sheet".

Decorated Mats

Decorative corners, hand-cut designs, and ink lines bring the spirit of their design to the matting presentation. Let the style, strength, and subject matter of the artwork guide decisions about the size, amount, and placement of decorative elements. Keep decorative elements within the first third of the mat border next to the window opening.

PROPORTION

Proportion is something one sees rather than measures. It is a personal visual perception of the balance of light, color, texture, shapes and line direction. When everything within a design has proper placement, size and intensity, good composition and balance of proportion have been achieved. Since mat borders can be made in a huge range of possible colors and dimensions, the matting is the most flexible element of the framing job.

Determining the "correct" amount of matting is largely a matter of personal preference. Every item to be matted should be seen as an individual design project. The color, style and size of the artwork will offer clues to help determine an appropriate design.

In general, avoid using very narrow mat borders, which can be distracting to the eye and do not provide enough transition space between artwork and frame. Do not be afraid to use large mat borders—they are often the key to good visual balance. It is especially important that decorative mats have sufficient borders to both accommodate the decoration and still provide that "breathing space" between artwork and frame.

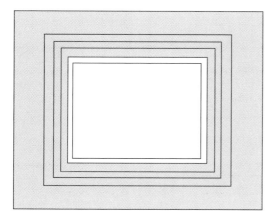

The decorative lines are overpowering and would be more prominent than the artwork.

A few decorative lines bring attention to the artwork, drawing the eye into the art.

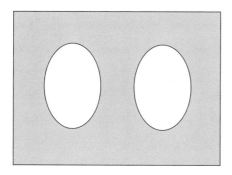

The border and the center width are the same. The ovals appear to separate.

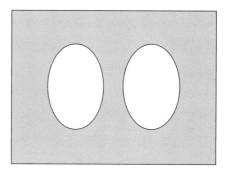

By reducing the center space between the ovals, the artwork appears centered. This arrangement provides good balance while featuring the artwork.

MAT BORDERS

Don't be afraid of large mat borders. They create a visually pleasing "breathing space" between the artwork and the frame. Small, narrow mats tend to distract the eye with patterns of lines going around the artwork.

Should the bottom of a mat be "weighted"? For some pieces it is the right thing to do, for others it is not. Cutting a mat with extra on the bottom was traditional in the past, based on several theories. Since the invention of the straight line mat cutter, it has been easiest to cut the borders equal on all sides. The even more recent advent of computer cutters allows the freedom to easily choose between equal and elongated mat borders.

Which looks better? Which is more appropriate? There is no single rule. It is a choice based on one's personal sense of proportion.

Look at examples in trade magazines, museums, home decoration magazines, homes and public spaces. Which matting styles make the art look important? What looks best on small pieces of art? Large pieces? Through experience framers learn how to make these choices with confidence. Feel free to experiment and try new designs.

Below are examples of mat openings with a variety of border sizes. Note the difference a border can make in the perception of size and importance.

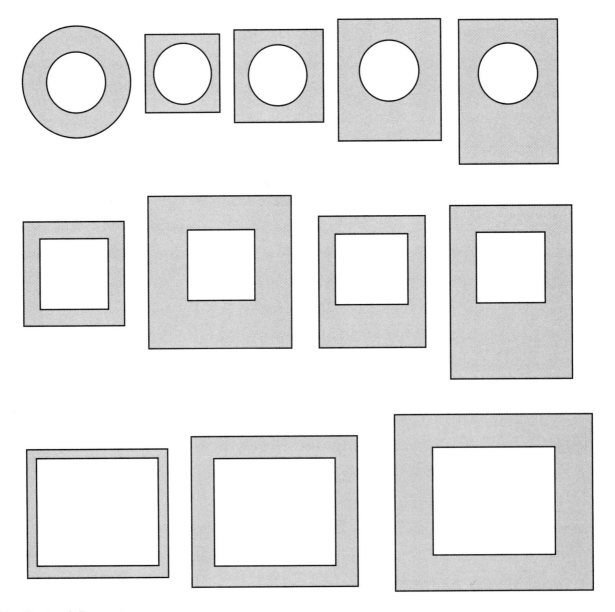

Practice helps to develop a sense of the proper size to make mat borders. Look at the examples on this page, showing different size borders around an 8x10" opening.

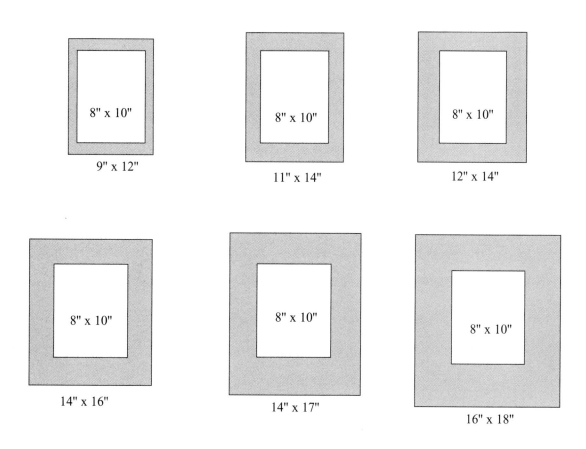

9" x 12"

11" x 14"

12" x 14"

14" x 16"

14" x 17"

16" x 18"

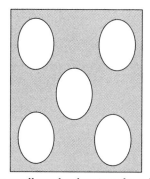

The small mat border gives these five ovals a closed, crowded feeling.

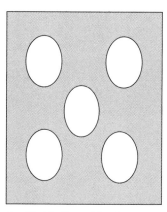

An inch added to the mat border surrounding the five ovals creates good balance.

COLOR

The study of color is a complex science involving psychology, physiology and physics. Basically (and I mean basically) color is light: we see color because of the various ways light is reflected and absorbed. In picture framing our concern is more with the psychology of color—the mood or visual effect created by different mat colors. Why do we prefer one color over another? How do we determine the "best" color for the artwork?

As in any matter involving more than one choice, there are differing schools of thought about color selection in matting. Ideas may come from the artwork to be matted, or from external sources, such as the environment in which the artwork will be hung. It is also helpful to understand the natural color relationships demonstrated by a color wheel.

First, some basic terminology:
> HUE refers to the name given to a color (red, blue, green, etc.)
>
> INTENSITY is the brightness (high intensity) or dullness (low intensity) of a hue.
>
> VALUE is the lightness or darkness of a hue in relation to black and white. Adding white to a hue raises the value and is called a TINT. Adding black to a hue lowers the value and is called a SHADE.

Look at the color wheel and consider the following principles: MONOCHROMATIC COLOR SCHEMES use one hue (color) in a range of values and intensities. These combinations are the most restful to the eye.

ANALOGOUS or RELATED COLORS are those that fall side-by-side on the color wheel. Except when the values are very intense, these colors are also relaxing to the eye.

COMPLEMENTARY COLORS are those that fall opposite one another on the color wheel. Using them together creates a very bold and vibrant effect. The impact is softened when one color dominates and the other is used as an accent.

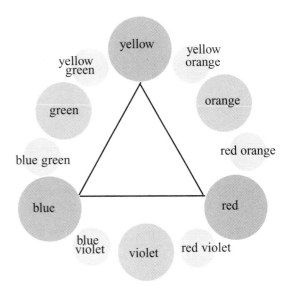

PRIMARY COLORS are:
> Red, Yellow and Blue

SECONDARY COLORS are
> Green, Orange and Violet

NEUTRALS are pure earth tones—browns, tans and grays. These tend to be subtle and can be used easily with other colors.

In the science of color, black and white are technically not colors. But in terms of matting, black and white are definitely strong color choices to be worked with carefully—they can be overwhelming when used in high contrast. To be successful, black or white mats must complement the artwork being matted.

By varying proportions and intensities, endless color combinations can be created.

Since decorative matting frequently requires using a variety of colors together, it is very helpful to sharpen your color skills. Experiment—practical experience is the best way to learn to manipulate color successfully.

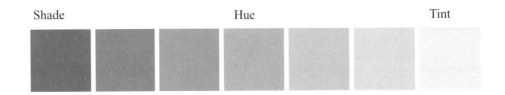

Shade   Hue   Tint

EQUIPMENT

CUTTING AND TRIMMING BOARDS

Mat and **mount boards must** be cut **accurately** for framing purposes. A board that is cut 1/16" off size will create problems throughout the frame job.

Boards can be trimmed on most straight line mat cutters or with a guillotine table model, or with a wall-mounted glass and board cutter.

The wall mount cutter is a practical and versatile machine that cuts matboards, mounting boards, and foam center boards as well as glass and plastic sheets. It is very simple to operate, and cuts materials squarely. Many models hold a glass cutting wheel, a board cutting blade, and a plastic cutter simultaneously on one head that spins to set the proper blade. A measuring rule is on the materials tray.

Table paper cutters are used by many framers to cut matboard and mounting boards. It was not meant to cut boards and will fight the effort, but with a little practice and a very firm grip, it will do the job. Of course, such heavy-duty use will make the cutter wear out faster and require frequent blade alignment. These cutters are available in several sizes; the 36" square is the most useful to a frame shop.

Table model board cutters are designed to cut thick boards accurately. They are better adapted to cutting framing materials than ordinary paper cutters.

The Keencut Excalibur wall-mounted cutter will cut glass, thick and thin boards, plastics and Masonite®.

The Fletcher 3000 can cut matboards, foam boards, glass, and plastic.

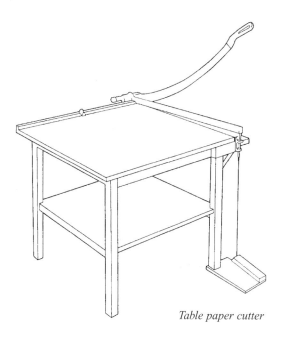

Table paper cutter

Mat Cutters

Anatomy of a "generic" straight line mat cutter.

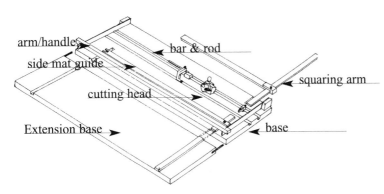

This illustration shows the basic elements of a straight line mat cutter, regardless of make or model.

Straight Line Mat Cutter

The straight line mat cutter has been an essential machine in frame shops for many years. A flat, sturdy base holds a cutting head that slides along a smooth metal bar. Replaceable blades attached to the head make bevel cuts and also straight cuts for blanking and trimming matboards. A straight line cutter cuts all types of square and rectangular mat openings, including angled cuts.

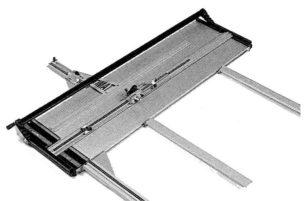

The KeenCut UltiMat Gold straight line mat cutter.

The Logan Framer's Edge straight line mat cutter.

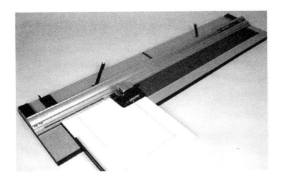

The Fletcher 2100 straight line mat cutter.

Oval Cutters

There were several models of oval cutters available to the professional picture framers, however, over the years the oval cutter has not been as popular. You may find several on the used market place such as the Oval Art, KeenCut, Fletcher, Circle Master and Artisan.

The C& H Advantage Pro straight line mat cutter.

The Logan Circle and Oval mat cutter.

The Esterly Speed-Mat.

ALL-PURPOSE MAT CUTTING SYSTEM

Cuts, matboard, glass, foam boards, can be upgraded to pneumatic plus it sizes boards and does v-grooves

The Speed-mat cutting system cuts four consecutive cuts without marking, touching or turning the mat. The controls make four perfect cuts, no over cuts, no run-ins or no run-outs

The base carriage is interchangeable with an option for cutting ovals and circles up to 28" x 36".

Borders are set using rule pointers on the baseboard. Production Stops/Spacers provide preset positions for precise offsets for cutting v-grooves, double and triple mats.

Esterly Standard can also be upgraded to a pneumatic knifehead for 4-ply mats. Pneumatic knifeheads engage, disengage and rotate with less effort than manual knifeheads.

VARIOUS ATTACHMENTS & ACCESSORIES

They may be several different attachments for the oval cutter to allow straight cuts, bevel cuts, embossing, inking and glass cutting.

Protractor style multi-angle attachment.

KeenCut offers multi-angle attachments that snap onto the straight line cutter.

There are several types of blades. It is important to use the correct blade with each cutter and to use the correct thickness of blade. A standard .012 (sometimes referred to as 1200) blade may be used to cut all types of matboard. A .015 blade is thicker, and may flex less when cutting thick boards.

A V-groover attachment for the Logan Framer's Edge.

COMPUTER MAT CUTTERS

These mat cutters use a computer and software connected to a cutting machine. They can cut most any kind of mat, once the software programs are mastered. Decorative corners, monograms, and lots of other specialty mat designs are part of the software programs, and most allow the operator to customize. The programs are often compatible with other popular frame shop software programs.

For the average frame shop, a computer mat cutter is an option, but not a necessity. Although the cost was once prohibitive for smaller frame shops, computer cutters have now become economically possible for many picture framers. There are numerous models available, and most offer leasing plans in addition to buying plans.

While computer cutters are particularly helpful in high production situations, even a shop with only moderate output can benefit from the ability to quickly produce intricate designs, multiple openings, and other special mats—without requiring a skilled framer. However, for a shop that cuts no more than ten to twenty mats per day, a traditional straight line mat cutter will be both efficient and economical. Fancy mats and large multiple openings can be "farmed-out" to distributors or other framers. The other choice would be to cut them your existing machines and, although it may take more time, you can cut most of the fancy mats the computer cutters produce. It depends on how many of these types of mats you will need during a years time.

Computer Mat Cutters
A mat blank is placed on the cutting machine. Matting options are viewed and selected on a computer monitor, then the software program instructs the machine to cut the chosen mat.

The framer designs the mat in the computer. Once satisfied with the measurements, the machine can be activated once the boards are put in position.

The framer has added two "cheater" rails to the side and bottom to reduce waste of matboard. She uses a removable tape to secure the mat to the rails. Then cuts the mat using the machine. The framer stays with the machine while it is cutting.

Mat Mathematics

Skill in using factions is very important in all phases of picture framing. Understanding the components of the inch is required to properly measure artwork and all parts of the framing package. A tiny fractional amount can be vital to the proper fit of all components of the framing. Do not try to "wing it" when it comes to fractions—they must be correct.

The inch is divided into equal parts. Fractions are pieces of an inch. Compare the illustrations on this page.

One inch.

1/2 means 1 of 2 equal pieces.

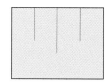

1/4 means 1 of 4 equal pieces.

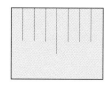

1/8 means 1 of 8 equal pieces.

A *fraction* of an inch
is a *part* of an inch.

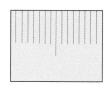

1/16 means 1 of 16 equal pieces.

1/16th of an inch means
the inch is divided into
16 equal sections,
and 1/16th represents
one section.

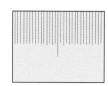

*1/32" means the inch has been broken into 32 equal pieces
and 1 part of it is being measured—1/32".*

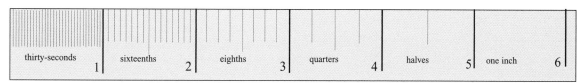

Fractions of an Inch on a Ruler.

Examples of Adding Simple Fractions

A.   2 1/2
    + 2 1/2

    first add 1/2 + 1/2 equals 1
    second add 2 + 2 equals 4
    then add 1 plus 4 equals 5
—or—
    1/2 + 1/2 = 1
    2 + 2 = 4
        1 + 4 = 5

Fractions can sometimes be "reduced" by dividing both numbers in the fraction by a common denominator, such as 2, 3 or 4. When fractions can be reduced, they should be; it makes them easier to work with.

    4/8 divided by 4 equals 1/2
    because 4 goes into the first number one time
        and into the second number 2 times
    2/4 divided by 2 equals 1/2
    8/16 divided by 8 equals 1/2
    12/16 divided by 4 equals 3/4
    6/16 divided by 2 equals 3/8
    6/8 divided by 2 equals 3/4

B.   3 1/4
    + 3 1/4

    first add 1/4 plus 1/4 equals 2/4
        2/4 is reduced to 1/2
    second add 3 plus 3 equals 6
    then add 6 plus 1/2 equals 6 1/2
—or—
    1/4 + 1/4 = 2/4 = 1/2
    3 + 3 = 6
        6 + 1/2 = 6 1/2

C.   3 1/8
    6 3/8
    + 3 1/8

    first add 1/8 plus 3/8 plus 1/8 equals 5/8
    second add 3 plus 6 plus 3 equals 12
    then add 12 plus 5/8 equals 12 5/8
—or—
    1/8 + 3/8 + 1/8 = 5/8
    3 + 6 + 3 = 12
        12 + 5/8 = 12 5/8

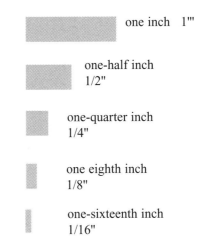

one inch   1'"

one-half inch
1/2"

one-quarter inch
1/4"

one eighth inch
1/8"

one-sixteenth inch
1/16"

These are examples of adding mixed fractions. Notice the conversion of some fractions to create a common denominator, making addition much easier:

    1 1/4   1 2/8
    + 2 5/8 or   2 5/8
              3 7/8

    11 7/8   11 7/8
    + 2 1/2 or   2 4/8
              13 11/8 = 14 3/8

    7 3/4   7 6/8
    + 3 5/8 or   3 5/8
              10 11/8 = 11 3/8

    1 3/16   1 3/16
    + 1 1/4 or   1 4/16
              2 7/16

The following fractions cannot be reduced. No single number can be divided into both numbers in the fraction. They must be used as is, in order to correctly express the exact measurement.

11/16   7/8   3/4   5/8   15/16   1/2   9/16

Mat Calculations

A. The artwork is 11x14" but it has a plate mark and signature which makes the required opening 12x141/2".

   The top and side borders are 3"
   The bottom measurement will be 3 1/2"

```
opening   12       x       14 1/2
         + 6 1/2                6
          18 1/2  x       20 1/2
```

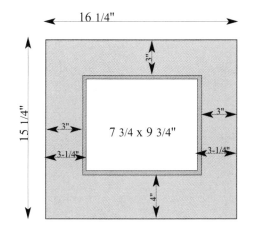

B. Two 5x7" photos in one frame.

The openings are 4 3/4" x 6 3/4"
The borders are 1 1/2"
The center space is 3/4"

Add the horizontal measurements:

```
    1 1/2  converts to    1 2/4
    4 3/4                  4 3/4
      3/4                               3/4
    4 3/4                  4 3/4
  + 1 1/2                + 1 2/4
          add together  10 13/4 or 13 1/4
```

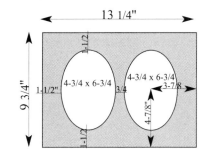

Add the vertical measurements:

```
    1 1/2  converts to    1 2/4
    6 3/4                  6 3/4
  + 1 1/2                + 1 2/4
                          8 7/4 or 9 3/4
```

C. Double matted 8x10" photo

The opening is 7 3/4" x 9 3/4"
The top mat border (top and sides) is 3"
   The bottom border is 4"
The second or undermat is 1/4" on all sides

Add the horizontal   Add the vertical
measurements: measurements:
```
      3                           3
        1/4                         1/4
      9 3/4                       7 3/4
        1/4                         1/4
    + 3                         + 4
    15 5/4 or 16 1/4            14 5/4 or 15 1/4
```

Writing a Work Order

Different shops use different systems for writing frame jobs on a work order. The most important thing is for the shop to have a system that everyone uses consistently.

Here is an example of a work sheet for an 8x10" photo with one 3" mat, regular glass, and a wire for hanging the frame.

Opening for photo: 7 3/4 x 9 3/4"
Mat border (3" x 2)   + 6   6
                        13 3/4 x 15 3/4"

For convenience, some framers like to round fractions up or down a bit to create whole numbers which are easier to deal with.

Perhaps the opening of the mat can be reduced or increased a small amount. Better yet, try adjusting the mat border. For example, if the 8x10" photo is given a 3 1/8" mat instead of a 3" mat, our frame size will be 14x16".

Opening for photo: 7 3/4 x 9 3/4
Mat border (3 1/8" x 2) + 6 1/4   6 1/4
                         14   x 16

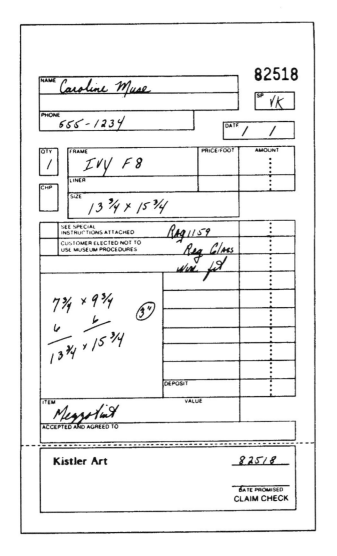

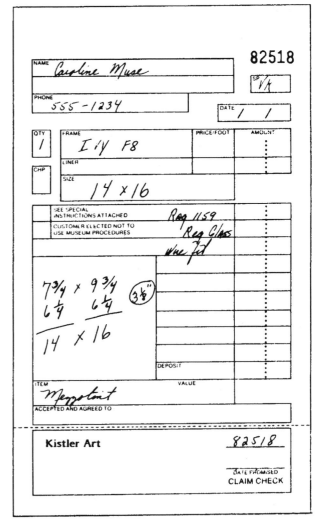

STANDARD SIZES

Because artwork is often made to standard sizes, glass is often pre-cut to standard sizes, and many ready-made frames are available in those sizes, it is important to know the standard sizes for the framing industry. Knowing these sizes can help when determining the size of a frame job. It is much easier to pull a lite of 16x20" glass out of a box and use it as is than to trim it to 15 7/8x19 7/8".

Remember your limitations. Matboards are available in 32x40". Some of the more popular colors are available in 40x60" and a few specialty manufacturers offer 4' x 8' in a few colors.

When any dimension exceeds the matboard size, creative mat cutting becomes important. Huge mats can be constructed by splicing, see pages 67-69.

The following is a list of the "standard" sizes commonly found in the art and framing industry.

4 x 5	11 x 14	24 x 36
4 x 6	12 x 16	26 x 32
5 x 7	14 x 18	30 x 40
6 x 8	16 x 20	32 x 40
8 x 10	18 x 24	36 x 48
8 x 12	20 x 24	40 x 48
8 1/2 x 11	22 x 28	40 x 60
9 x 12	24 x 30	48 x 96

ANGLES

A simple protractor will help when making multiple-sided mats or frames.

The following are a few reference angles used by picture framers. Mat cutters may have optional angle attachments.

Art papers have their own system of standard sizes. Some trade names and their sizes are:

Imperial	22 x 30"
Royal	19 x 24"
Super-Royal	19 1/4 x 27"
Elephant	23 x 28"
Double Elephant	26 1/2 x 40"
Antiquarian	31 x 53"

METRICS

There are two standard systems of measurement—Metric and British. The Metric system is used throughout much of the world while the British system is only used by the United States and a few small countries.

The standard unit of measure for the Metric system is the meter (approximately 39 3/8"). The standard for the British system is the foot (30.48cm).

Although the British system is used throughout this book, the following comparisons and the accompanying conversion list may be helpful.

A Millimeter(mm) is 1/1000th of a meter or .001
A Centimeter(cm) is 1/100th of a meter or .01
1 Inch equals 2.54(cm) or 2540mm
1 Foot equals 30.48(cm) or 304.8mm

British Inches	Millimeters	Centimeters
1/32	.7937	
1/16	1.5875	
1/8	3.175	
3/16	4.7625	
1/4	6.35	
3/8	9.525	
1/2	12.7	1.27
5/8	15.875	1.58
3/4	19.05	1.90
7/8	22.225	2.22
1	25.4	2.54
1-1/4	31.75	3.17
1-2/2	38.1	3.81
1-3/4	44.45	4.44
2	50.8	5.08
2-1/4	57.15	5.71
2-1/2	63.5	6.35
2-3/4	69.85	6.98
3	76.2	7.62
3-1/4	82.55	8.25
3-1/2	88.90	8.89
3-3/4	95.25	9.52
4	101.60	10.16
4-1/4	107.95	10.79
4-1/2	114.30	11.43
4-3/4	120.65	12.06
5	127.00	12.7

To convert from millimeters to centimeters move the decimal point one digit to the left.
Example: 55.0 millimeters = 5.5 centimeters

Standard sizes converted from
Inches to Millimeters

5 x 7	127.0 x 177.8
8 x 10	203.2 x 254.0
9 x 12	228.6 x 304.8
11 x 14	279.4 x 355.6
12 x 16	304.8 x 406.1
14 x 18	355.6 x 508.0
16 x 20	406.1 x 508.0
18 x 24	457.2 x 609.6
20 x 24	508.0 x 609.6
22 x 28	558.8 x 711.2
24 x 30	609.6 x 762.0
24 x 36	609.6 x 914.0
32 x 40	812.8 x 1016.0
36 x 48	914.4 x 1219.2
40 x 60	1016.0 x 1524.0

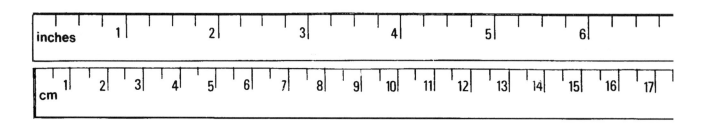

TYPES OF BOARDS

BOARDS FOR CUTTING MATS

Matboards are manufactured specifically for picture framing. Regardless of the design of the mat or the value of the artwork, matboards are the only appropriate materials for mats made by professional picture framers.

Most matboards are made from layers of paper pasted or laminated together to form a sheet. Solid cotton rag matboards are formed into a solid sheet of compressed pulp. The thickness of boards was traditionally measured in points or plys, and these standards of measure can often be seen in literature from manufacturers of the boards. Points and plys are rarely discussed by picture framers, except to designate solid rag matboards, which are typically available in 2-ply, 4-ply, 6-ply and 8-ply thicknesses.

MATBOARDS

ACID-FREE REGULAR MATBOARD

This is the minimum quality matboard suitable for professionals. It is standard wood pulp matboard buffered with calcium carbonate to neutralize the acids present in the materials. It is made from layers of paper, with a surface paper that carries the color, and a white lining paper attached to the back of the board. A wide selection of colors and surface patterns is available. The neutral pH level is long-lasting, and the surface colors tend to be stable, but this board is intended for decorative framing, not for conservation, because of the acidic wood pulp core.

WHITE CORE MATBOARD

A few companies have introduced a line of non-conservation white core matboards. These boards offer the design appeal of a crisp white bevel at a lower cost than rag or conservation board. Despite their attractive appearance, these boards are not conservation quality and are not intended for conservation framing.

RAG MATBOARD

Rag matboard is made of 100% pure cotton fiber. "Rag" is a papermaker's term from centuries ago when cotton rags and trimmings were the principal raw material for paper-making. Cotton is still used to make the finest papers and matboards.

Cotton is naturally white and acid-free, so little processing is required. Rag matboard is usually buffered with calcium carbonate or a similar agent to provide a buffer against environmental acids. It is strong and stable, and has a proven history. Rag matboard has been relied upon by museums since the 1930s. It is available in 2-ply, 4-ply, 6-ply, and 8-ply thicknesses. The 2-ply is too thin to use for mats.

Solid rag matboards are made from compressed pulp, rather than layers of paper. The color selection is limited, consisting mainly of neutral and pastel colors, because the coloring agent has to meet conservation requirements and must color the cotton fibers evenly.

UNBUFFERED RAG MATBOARD

This 100% cotton board is the same as 4-ply rag matboard, except it has no buffering. It is made for photographs and other artwork requiring a non-alkaline environment. Buffering creates an alkaline environment, and excessive alkali can cause an adverse reaction with some photographs, some textiles, and a few other types of art.

CONSERVATION MATBOARDS

These boards are made with a rag or purified woodpulp core, and have surface papers adhered to the core. The surface papers are acid-free and highly fade- and bleed-resistant. The lining papers on the back of the board are also acid-free. The boards are buffered. For conservation framing, this board is nearly as good as 100% rag board. The boards made from purified wood pulp are often called alpha cellulose boards. The wood pulp is processed until no acidic lignin remains.

CONSERVATION BOARDS WITH MOLECULAR TRAPS

One type of matboard contains additives called "zeolites," which are "cage molecules" designed to attract, trap, and neutralize a range of pollutants beyond those dealt with by buffering agents. This product may well be a valuable tool for conservation framing; lab tests have shown promising results, especially in dealing with high levels of air pollution. Some conservators are concerned about the long-term effects of active ingredients like zeolites within the frame package.

FABRIC-COVERED MATBOARDS

There are many matboards available covered with fabric. Many of them are acid-free. Check manufacturer's specifications for details about pH content and fade-resistance.

BRITECORES®, BLACK CORES, AND COLOR CORES

These boards are made from chemically-processed wood pulp and are saturated with pigment. Some are suitable for conservation, some are not. Check with the manufacturer for pH, buffering, and lignin content.

FOAM CENTER BOARD

Foam board typically consists of a polystyrene core with paper laminated to the front and back surfaces. It is lightweight, rigid, and resists moisture. The surface papers may be buffered rag, buffered acid-free, or wood pulp. Use the rag or acid-free surfaces in conservation framing.

Foam board is intended mainly for use as a mounting or filler board, but it can also be used as a base for a fabric or paper-covered mat, as a spacer, or as a support in a sink mat. MightyCore® is a very dense foam board and can be used to make deep bevel mats.

Although the polystyrene core of foam center board can deteriorate and off-gas if exposed to light, it is considered inert when sealed inside of a frame.

Mounting boards and other boards used in picture framing are not suitable for mats, either because of their composition or because their core will not make an attractive bevel.

Warping while in storage can be a problem with boards used in picture framing. Note that boards warp more in the direction of their grain. The grain can usually be determined by standing a board on its short end, observing the degree of bowing, then standing the board on its long end, comparing this amount of bowing to that of the other edge. The bowing will be greater when the grain is parallel to the floor. Store the boards standing on the side opposite their grain.

HINT: When boards get scuffed from brushing against each other, dampen a clean sponge with clean water and gently wipe across the scuff. The moisture will help to raise the fibers that were smashed down. This method will also clean a dusty board.

This reproduction is triple-matted using decorative matboards with a marble pattern.

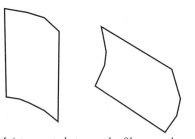

Moisture gets between the fibers on the grain and expands the board, causing it to warp.

CONSERVATION MATTING

Conservation matting involves specialized materials and methods. Any cutting technique or decoration style may be used, as long as the materials and methods meet conservation standards.

CONSERVATION RULES FOR MATTING:

• The board used for the window mat and for the backing board directly behind the art must be Rag or Conservation matboard. The backing board should be the same type of board as is used for the mat.

• The art should be attached to the backing board. To position the art on the backing board: Place the art on the backing board. Place the mat on top of the art. Position the art correctly in the mat opening. Place a clean weight on the art to maintain its position. Remove the mat. Attach the art to the backing board.

• The method used to attach the art to the backing board is an essential part of conservation framing. There are several options, but all must meet the same criteria: clean, stable, acid-free, and completely reversible with no harm to the artwork.

• Japanese paper hinges, gummed linen or paper hinges, mounting strips, troughs, and pocket corners are the most common attachment methods.

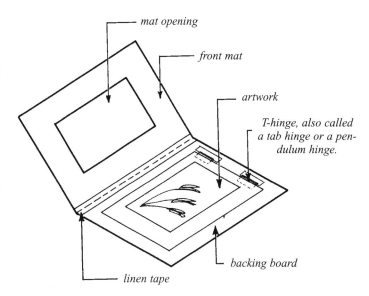

mat opening

front mat

artwork

T-hinge, also called a tab hinge or a pendulum hinge.

backing board

linen tape

Pass-through Hinge

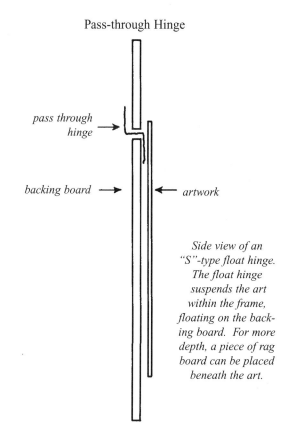

pass through hinge

backing board → ← *artwork*

Side view of an "S"-type float hinge. The float hinge suspends the art within the frame, floating on the backing board. For more depth, a piece of rag board can be placed beneath the art.

V- Hinge

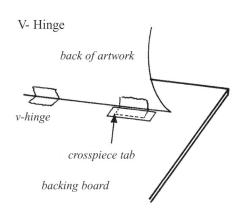

back of artwork

v-hinge

crosspiece tab

backing board

PROBLEMS AND SOLUTIONS

CUTTING PROBLEMS

HOOK AT BEGINNING OF CUT

- Improper stance. Stand at the base of the cutter, wrist and arm free to pull straight back.
- Slip sheet (underlayment) may be worn—the blade gets caught in the cuts.
- Blade extended too far. It should penetrate the matboard and just "score" the slip sheet.
- Blade is dull or wrong thickness.

NOTCH

- Indentations in the first 1/4" of the cut are caused by the operator hesitating while inserting the blade. Enter the board with one smooth stroke.
- The cutting head is lurching forward upon entry, pushing the dull part of the blade into the board.

CURVE ON SIDE OF MAT OPENING

- Mat cutter is not level, allowing the base to bow thus lifting the blade.
- Slip sheet is too short for size of mat cutter. This causes the rod and bar to bend.
- Slip sheet is too narrow, causing the rod and bar to tilt. Slip sheets should be at least 6" wide and at least 2/3 of the length of the cutter.

MAT BORDERS NOT EVEN WIDTH

- Side of mat guide must be perfectly parallel to the rod and bar and perpendicular to the bottom mat guide.
- The arm must not have any play. When opening and closing the cutter the arm and hinges must not be loose. Tighten or replace loose hinges.

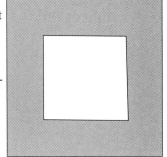

MATBOARD SLIPS UNDER BAR

- The cutter must be placed on a perfectly flat table base.

RAGGED CUTS

- Change the blade.
- Use a slip sheet to eliminate rough cuts altogether.
- An emery board can be used to file rough cuts.

OVERCUTS

- Use a slip sheet to eliminate rough cuts altogether. Typical solutions include burnishing to push the cut fibers in place, or taping the underside of the cut to conceal the overcut. However, over time these methods do not effectively conceal the cut. If the mat experiences a climate change (in or out of the frame) the board fibers can expand and contract, revealing the overcut.

UNDERCUTS

- From the front of the mat, slide a single edge razor blade into the corner at an angle to complete the cut. Often a rough edge will be visible.

TILTED OVAL CUTS

- May be caused by too much pressure while rounding off the top or the side holders may be shifting.

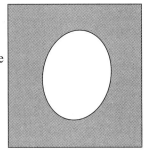

MATBOARD PROBLEMS

OUT OF SQUARE MATS

- Both the board cutter and the mat cutter **must** be perfectly square! Both machines have adjustments to correct alignment. Use a carpenters square to check for **perfect** alignment. Square all the machines at least once a week.

BLOOD ON MATBOARDS

- Let dry and scrape off with a razor blade.
- Wash off with your own saliva. Your saliva is a solvent for your blood.
- Throw out the mat and start again!

PENCIL SMEARS ON BACK OF MATS

- Use a hard lead pencil, which will make a thinner, lighter line—easier to erase if you use a light touch, or use measuring stops to avoid the need for pencil marks. Erase any pencil marks with a white vinyl eraser.

SCUFFED MATBOARD

- Wipe lightly with a damp sponge.

WHITE GLUE ON VELVET MATS

- Use white vinegar as a solvent.

GREASE ON MATBOARDS
- The best solution is to throw the board away and start over, because no matter how you try to remove it or cover it, the stain will reappear at a later date.

NAP OF FABRIC CRUSHED
- Steam with an iron, keeping the iron above the surface of the fabric. Use a spacer to keep the fabric away from the glass.

PRODUCTS COMMONLY USED
WHEN CUTTING MATS

810 TAPE: A clear, stable, non-staining, permanent tape made by 3M Company. Also called Magic Mending Tape.

811 TAPE: A clear, stable, non-staining, light adhesive tape made by 3M Company. The adhesive is similar to "Post-it" notes. Easy to remove from most surfaces.

ATG Tape: 3M's #924 tape is double-sided adhesive tape usually dispensed from an Adhesive Transfer Gun.

BLADES: There are several types of mat cutter blades; framing supply distributors may offer several that fit each machine. Some blades have a single edge (ground to a sharp bevel on just one side, it flexes less and may last longer), others have a double edge; experiment to determine personal preference. Blades are offered in various thicknesses, to cut through thin and thick boards, but a .012 standard blade (often referred to as 1200 by manufacturers) may be used for cutting all types of matboard, adjusting the blade depth as necessary. PERFECT MOUNT FILM: A sheet of double-sided adhesive between sheets of release paper. Repositionable and pH-neutral. Permanent bond develops in 8-24 hours.

PMA: Positional Mounting Adhesive is a sheet of double-sided adhesive between sheets of release paper.

LINEN TAPE: A 100% cotton tape available with either a pressure-sensitive or water-activated adhesive.

BURNISHER: A round-ended tool that uses the operator's hand-pressure to indent or smooth an area on a mat. Often used in an attempt to conceal overcuts.

MYLAR: A clear flexible sheet that looks like acetate but is actually 100% clear polyester. The type mentioned in this book is uncoated, untreated, 3 or 4 mil. Mylar D.

MATTING TERMINOLOGY

WINDOW MAT: a piece of matboard with an opening cut for the purpose of displaying art or objects.

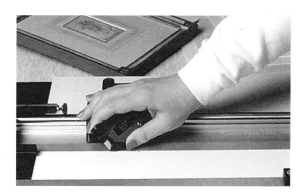

MAT PACKAGE: a window mat and a backing board made from the same type of board as the mat

TOP MAT: this is the uppermost window mat in a multiple layer mat such as double mat, triple mat, etc.

UNDERMAT, BOTTOM MAT, LOWER MAT: this is the bottom layer of a multiple layer mat. In a triple mat there is also a middle mat.

LIP, LINER, REVEAL: these terms refer to the strip of matting exposed in the window opening of a top mat in double, triple, and other multiple layer mats.

BLADE DEPTH:
Proper blade depth is essential when cutting mats. Test and adjust the blade depth any time a different type of matboard is cut. The difference in thickness between a regular matboard and a fabric-covered matboard—or between a 4-ply rag matboard and a black core matboard—is enough to cause overcuts, undercuts, or ragged cuts if the blade depth is not correct for the board. When properly set, the blade should cut entirely through the matboard and just scratch the slip sheet underneath. (See Slip Sheet, page 29).

CUTTING UP A MATBOARD

Matboards are typically available in two sizes: 32x40", and 40x60". Some are available even larger, such as 48x96". The most common size is 32x40". Matboards are usually slightly larger than the size noted. This extra bit allows for expansion and contraction during manufacture, shipping and storage and also guarantees a framer can get a perfectly square 32x40" board from the sheet.

When ordering boards, it is important to consider how many mats and corresponding backing boards can be cut from a sheet. Most frame shops waste a lot of matboard. If a 20x24" is cut, there is still enough for another 20x24" (the backing, or a second mat). However, if a 22x28" is cut, there won't be enough for another and backing will have to be cut from a second board. Don't forget to include this in pricing.

In daily practice, framers are seldom able to use a whole board economically, because the typical frame job is for one custom frame. However, any time a board is being cut, consideration should be given to making the cuts in a way that maximizes the usable scrap that remains.

Scrap board can be used for slip sheets in the mat cutter, and for backing boards in frame jobs. Even so, excess scrap matboard accumulates. After a while they must be thinned out or disposed of. Donate them to a school or recycle them.

Note: When using a computer mat cutter, the calculations at the right may not work. The computer mat cutter may require more area because of the positioning of the blades and the grips.

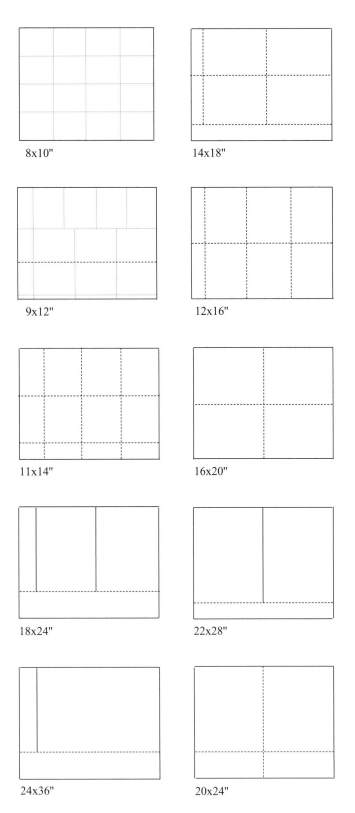

8x10"   14x18"

9x12"   12x16"

11x14"   16x20"

18x24"   22x28"

24x36"   20x24"

CHAPTER TWO

MAT CUTTING

Mat cutting is an art. It requires skill which can be developed with practice. Skill, combined with quality materials and a perfectly aligned machine are the tools needed for artistic mat cutting.

Read the owner's manual that came with the mat cutter, and make adjustments and calibrations as needed to get the cutter in optimum condition. The payoff is an efficient machine that produces the results expected, saving wasted time and materials—and racked nerves.

CHECKLIST
• Make sure the baseboard is fully supported and level
• Square up the following to the bar and rod:
    mat guide (side)
    bottom mat guide
    squaring arm
• Check the depth of the blade
• Use a slip sheet
• Use sharp blades
• Stand at the base of the cutter
• Put full, even pressure on the cutting head
• Do not jab the blade into the matboard
• Dry out damp boards in the heat press before cutting

BASIC DIRECTIONS
Most mats shown in this text have an outside dimension of 11x14". The border will typically be 3". This size allows the mats to serve as samples for the frame shop. The sample mats may be left intact, or cut at the upper right and lower left corners to make corner samples.

Most of the mats in the following projects have the same amount of border on all four sides. If a weighted-bottom mat is preferred, trim 1/2" off the top and sides after the mat is completed. Although the colors used in matting are essential to the design, black, white, and gray are used here to simplify the directions.

THE SLIP SHEET
A slip sheet is a strip of scrap matboard that rests beneath the mat during cutting. It helps to hold the matboard firmly in position and guides the cutting blade, providing clean cuts. The slip sheet should be about six inches wide and at least 2/3 the length of the cutter. The cutting blade should be set to cut entirely through the matboard, then just scratch the slip sheet. Use a slip sheet whenever possible. Replace the slip sheet when it becomes ragged from too many cuts.

Skill, combined with quality materials and a perfectly aligned machine are the tools needed for artistic mat cutting.

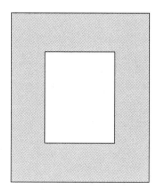

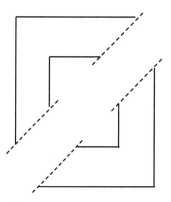

Make 3" or wider sample mats, then cut them to make two corner samples.

*Use a **slip sheet** anytime a single layer of matboard is being cut.*

How To Cut a Single Opening Mat
Pencil Scribed Method

1. Cut a matboard to the exact outside measurements.

2. Adjust the side mat guide for the correct border size. **Insert a slip sheet.**

3. Stand at the bottom of the cutter and lift the handle; place the matboard **face down** on the slip sheet.

4. Hold the matboard firmly against the edge of the mat guide.

5. Using a pencil, draw a line that will act as a guide for the cutter head. Draw lightly on all four sides, over-lapping the lines at the corners. The intersecting lines show where to start and stop the cut.

6. Slide the cutting head up to the top of the mat.

7. Place right hand on the cutter head. The first two fingers will provide the "power".

8. Position the blade approximately 3/16" above the inter-secting lines. Push down on the blade with two fingers, taking care to insert the blade smoothly rather than jabbing it into the board. Note: the head may surge forward causing a dent or punch on the front corner. Hold the head still when inserting into the matboard to avoid this problem.

9. Slide the cutting head down until it reaches the lower intersection. Pass the intersection by 3/16" then release the cutter head—it will pop up.

10. Lift the handle slightly with the left hand while turning the matboard to the next side with the right hand, then cut the second side as the first.

11. Continue around the four sides, taking care the fallout (or dropout) does not tear at the corners.

12. If there are "short cuts" on the mat, do not remove the fallout, or the unfinished corner will tear. Instead, slip a single edge razor blade through the face of the mat, at the same angle as the cut, and finish the cut to the corner.

To prevent marks on the face of the artwork, erase the pencil lines on the back of the mat.

5

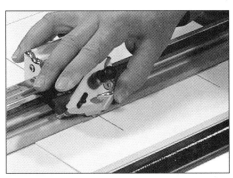

8

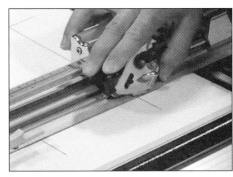

9

11

USING MEASURING STOPS

Many mat cutters are equipped with measuring stops, either attached to the cutting head (called a traveling stop) or as separate pieces that attach to the guide rail of the cutter.

The stops determine where the cuts will start and stop, without the need for pencil marks or calculating where to begin and end the cut.

Once considered appropriate only for production work, in which large numbers of identical mats must be cut quickly, many custom framers have found that using stops is quick and easy even for individual mats.

Properly calibrated stops control where each cut begins and ends, creating clean, crisp corners without overcuts. The manufacturer's instruction booklet should explain how to calibrate the stops for your machine.
Stops are useless if they are not calibrated.

CUTTING A MAT USING TRAVELING STOPS

1. Insert a slip sheet.

2. Set the side mat guide, the top stop and the bottom stop to 3".

3. Lift handle and place an 11x14" matboard **face down** in the cutter, resting against the side mat guide and the bottom mat guide.

4. Place the top stop so it rests against the top edge of the matboard.

5. Insert the blade into the board—smoothly, without jabbing or lurching forward. Once the blade is in the board, allow the top stop to lift up. Pull the cutting head down until it reaches the bottom stop.

6. Rotate the board to the next side and repeat the process until all four side are cut.

Do not slam the cutting head against the bottom stop—it may cause shifting, resulting in an incorrect cut.

3

4

5

Pull the cutting head down until it reaches the bottom stop.

Cutting a Mat Using
Three-piece Measuring Stops

1. Set side mat guide, top stop and bottom stop to 3".

2. Insert a slip sheet.

3. Lift handle and place an 11x14" matboard **face down** in the cutter, resting against the side mat guide and the bottom mat guide.

4. Place the stop arm so it rests against the top edge of the matboard.

5. Slide the cutting head up to the top stop, until it rests against the stop. Do not slam the cutting head against the top or bottom stop—it may cause them to move, resulting in an incorrect cut.

6. Insert the blade into the board—smoothly, without jabbing. Pull the cutting head down until it reaches the bottom stop.

7. Rotate the board to the **opposite** side to make the second cut.

8. Rotate the board to an uncut side and cut.

9. Rotate to the opposite side and complete the mat.

With a cutter that has a separate piece for a top stop, cut the two long sides, then the two short sides.

Adjust the border width measurement on the stop arm.

Double Mats

Double mats allow a narrow strip of matting (called a reveal) to accent the inner edge of the main mat. There are two approaches to cutting double mats.

Method A: Two Separate Boards

For this method, it is important that the two mat "blanks" are equal to one another in size. Cut the bottom mat, the one that will rest directly on the artwork, first. This bottom mat is also called the "undermat" or "liner mat." Measure and cut this as any single mat. To figure the window size of the top mat, which will be cut separately, use the opening and border size of the liner as the guide. Decide how much of the undermat is going to show—frequently 1/4" each side, but it may be 1/8", 1/2", or some other amount each side. The top mat border will be that much smaller than the undermat border on each side. Then do the addition.

Example: The opening for the artwork measures 8x10". The mat will have a 3" border each side.

So: 8" x 10"   opening for liner mat
    + 6   6"   3" border each side
     14" x 16"   outside size for liner mat

The mat will have a 1/4" reveal showing on all sides.

So: 8"   x 10"   liner opening
  +   1/2"   1/2"   1/4" reveal each side
     8 1/2" x 10 1/2"   opening for top mat

The top mat has a 2 3/4" border.

Now that the opening for the top mat is determined, determine the mat borders in the usual way:

    8 1/2"   x 10 1/2"   opening for top mat
  + 5 1/2"   5 1/2"   2 3/4" border each side
    14"   x 16"   outside size

Some find it easier to think of it this way:
    The undermat border is 3" each side, and 1/4" of this border will show all around; so subtract 1/4" from 3" = 2 3/4" border.

Cut one 14x16" board for the top mat.
Cut one 14x16" board for the under mat.
Then cut the openings in the two boards.

The undermat has a 3" border.

METHOD B: THE PERFECT DOUBLE MAT TEMPLATE METHOD

When the mat and liner are cut separately, the two openings do not always align with each other evenly. With the template method, the liner mat is attached to the top mat during cutting, which ensures two parallel openings. The edges of only the top mat touch the mat guide during the cutting of both layers.

1. Trim the top matboard to 14x16". Cut a 2 3/4" border in this mat. Save the fallout from the center of the mat.

2. Trim the undermat board to approximately 13 3/4" x 15 3/4". Apply a short piece of double-sided tape to all four sides of the surface of the undermat. Adhere the top mat to the undermat board with the front of the undermat board against the back of the top mat.

3. Apply a small strip of double-sided tape to the back of the fallout piece, and replace it in the mat opening, pressing to adhere it to the undermat board. The fallout creates a level cutting surface and also serves as a slip sheet.

4. Set the double board unit **face down** in the cutter. Set the cutter for a 3" border. Cut all four sides. The fallout will drop away, leaving a perfectly cut double mat.

This method works because the edges of the top mat serve as a template for the undermat; this assures the two openings will be evenly aligned and parallel to one another.

Although smaller board pieces may be used for liner mats (since only a small amount will show), this practice is not recommended, because the "dropoff" where the undermat ends may cause buckling in the fit job. This buckling may be apparent right away, or may happen gradually as the framing hangs on the customer's wall.

The methods described for cutting double mats are also used to cut triple mats, etc.

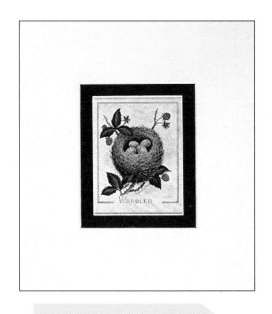

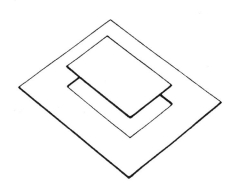

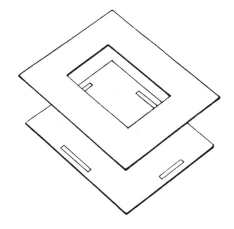

TRIPLE MATS

The triple mat, with its inner lip of a matching or contrasting color, is a mainstay of professional mat cutting. The template cutting method, in which the boards are attached to one another during cutting, is used to ensure parallel borders.

MATERIALS:
Three matboards 11x14"
    Lt. Gray top mat   2 3/4" border
    Dk. Gray middle mat 3" border
    Lt. Gray undermat 3 3/4" border
    Double-sided tape

1. Set the mat guides to 2 3/4".
   Cut the Lt. Gray 11x14" top mat.

2. Trim 1/4" off two sides of the Dk. Gray board.

3. Using double-stick tape, attach the Dk. Gray to the underside of the Lt. Gray top mat. Replace the fallout.

4. Remove the slip sheet from the cutter.

5. Set the mat guides to 3". Place the two attached boards in the cutter **face down** and cut the 3" border.

6. Trim 1/4" from the third matboard (Lt. Gray).

7. Attach the Lt. Gray board to the underside of the stack.

8. Set mat guides to 3 3/4".

9. Place the stack of three matboards **face down** back into the mat cutter and cut the mat. Remove the fall-outs.

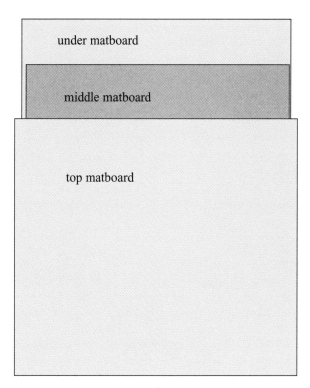

Weighted Bottom Mats

This mat typically has equal borders on the top and sides, with extra width on the bottom border. The amount of weight may be slight or moderate, appearing balanced when viewed.

Often considered a traditional style, the weighted bottom mat is often the best style mat to use on many works of art. Whether rooted in the Victorian tradition of hanging pictures very high on the wall, or in response to a natural visual preference for a solid base, this style is an attractive design option for most traditional art.

Cutting a weighted bottom mat

1. Set side mat guide to 3".

2. Place matboard in cutter **face down** and mark the top and sides with a pencil.

3. Move the mat guide to 4".

4. Place the matboard **face down** in the cutter. Pencil mark the 4" border then cut that side.

5. Return the mat guide to 3" and cut the remaining three sides.

Another option is to cut the mat with 4" borders on all four edges, then trim 1" off the top and sides.

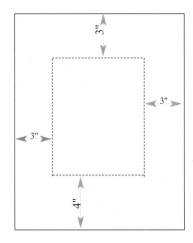

Museum Style Matting

An exaggerated weighted bottom has a distinctly different look from the slightly weighted bottom. The art is often placed in the upper area leaving a very large lower margin. Often museums use this style when mounting a collection of different size pieces using frames of uniform size. This style is suitable for 8x10" photos as well as very small images.

INLAY MAT

MATERIALS:
White matboard, 11x14"
Gray matboard, 10 3/4x13 3/4"
Double-sided tape
3M #810 tape

1. Place a 1" strip of double-sided tape on the face of the Gray board, near the outside edge of all four sides. Place the White board **face up** on the Gray board, and press to adhere to the double-sided tape.

2. Set the mat guide and stops to 3".

3. Place the two layers of board in the cutter, **face down** Cut a 3" border on all four sides. The pieces will stay together.

4. Remove the stops and set the mat guide to 2 1/2".

5. Insert the two layers in the cutter **face down** and slice all the way from top to bottom of all four sides. The Gray corners will fall away. Remove the taped side pieces. The remaining Gray rectangle is the inlay.

6. With the guide still set to 2 1/2", insert the White mat matboard **face down** in the cutter and cut an ordinary window mat. Discard the fallout.

7. Connect the two mats. Place the White mat **face down** on the worktable. Insert the Gray inlay **face down** and tape it to the mat with #810 tape on all four sides.

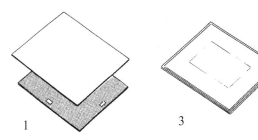

1

3

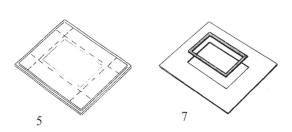

5

7

Single Inlay

Double Inlay(insert)

DIPLOMA MAT WITH
SPLICED SCHOOL COLORS

MATERIALS:
White matboard, 11x14"
Two scrap matboards, 8x8",
    Lt. Gray, Dk. Gray
Mat angle guide or 45-degree angle
3M #810 tape

1. Cut one piece of White matboard 11x14". Cut two scraps of matboard at least 8x8", choosing the school colors. This example will use Lt. Gray and Dk. Gray.

2. Use an angle template set at 3 1/4" to slice the lower left corner off all three boards. As an alternative to the angle template, use a 45-degree angle to measure 4", then trim all three boards.

3. Discard the Lt. and Dk. Gray corners, save the White one.

4. Set the mat guide to 1/2". Insert the White board **face up** at a 45-degree angle, and trim 1/2". Repeat the procedure with the other two boards.

5. Repeat the 1/2" trimming procedure on all three boards.

6. Assemble the spliced corner, using #810 tape on the back of the mat. Attach the Lt. Gray strip to the White mat, attach the Dk. Gray strip to the Lt. Gray strip, then attach the White corner piece to the Lt. Gray strip.

•Note: The splicing can be done with three colors, four colors—as many as desired. Simply follow the steps above, using a board for each color.

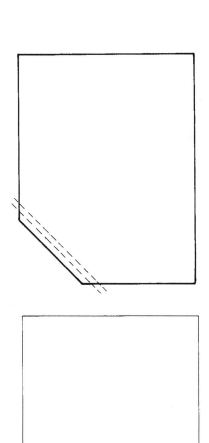

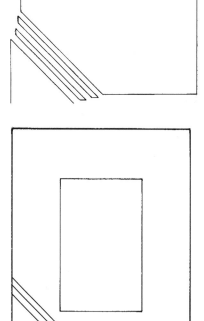

OFFSET CORNER

MATERIALS:
One matboard 11x14"

1. Set the side mat guide to 3" and the top and bottom stops to 3 1/4".

2. Insert the matboard in the cutter **face down** and cut the four sides. The center will not fall out.

3. Reset the mat guide to 3 1/4" and the top and bottom stops to 3".

4. Insert the board **face down** and cut the four sides, releasing the center piece.

Changing the size of the offset will change the style of the mat. The offset may look Art Deco or like an Indian motif depending on the size and color.

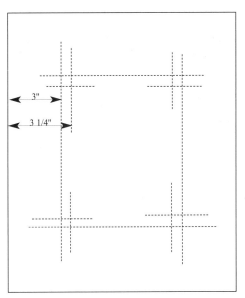

COMBINING AN OFFSET WITH A SINGLE MAT
Using a single mat over or under an offset corner will dramatically change the design.

DOUBLE OFFSET CORNER:

MATERIALS:
Two matboards:
  White 11x14" for top mat
  Gray 10 3/4" x 13 3/4" for undermat
  Double-sided tape

1. Set the mat guide to 2 3/4". Set the stops to 3 ".

2. Place White matboard in the cutter **face down**. Cut all four sides; the center will not fall out.

3. Reset the mat guide to 3" and the stops to 2 3/4".

4. Cut all four sides; the center will drop out. Save it.

5. Apply a short strip of double-sided tape near the outer edge of all four sides of the face of the Gray board. Attach the White mat to the Gray board, making sure none of the Gray board extends beyond the edges of the White.

6. Replace the White fallout in the mat opening, attaching it to the Gray board with a small strip of double-sided tape.

7. Place the two boards in the cutter **face down** and cut all four sides.

8. Reset the mat guide to 3 1/4" and the stops to 3" and cut all four sides. The fallout will fall out.

V-Groove Mats

V-grooves are decorative lines cut into the matboard by directing two bevels towards one other, creating a "V"-shaped groove. Usually used to make a line that traces around the mat opening, V-grooves can also be helpful when splicing oversized mats (see page 68.) The three methods described here make a single V-groove, but the process can be repeated as often as the design dictates.

The Traditional Method I

MATERIALS:
One matboard 11x14"
Hard pencil
#810 tape

1. Set the mat guide and stops to 2 1/2".

2. Make a pencil mark on the back of the board as illustrated. This permits the fallout to be replaced in its correct alignment.

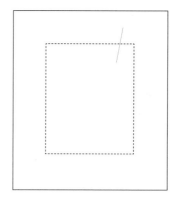

3. Cut the 2 1/2" border on all four sides. This makes one side of the V-groove. Set the mat aside.

4. Place the fallout **face up** beneath the mat cutter bar so it extends 1/8" to the left of the blade. Make sure it is 1/8"—if less is trimmed off, the fallout will not fit back in the opening; if too too much is trimmed off there will be a gap. Cut a bevel on all four sides of the fallout. This will take practice.

5. Place the trimmed fallout back into the mat opening, matching up the pencil mark. Tape with #810 tape on all four sides. The V-groove is now complete.

6. Place the mat in the cutter **face down** and cut a 3" border on all four sides.

There are V-groove attachments available from some mat cutter companies that make cutting v-grooves easy.

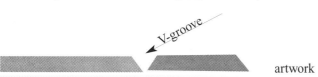

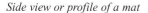
Side view or profile of a mat

V-GROOVE METHOD II

MATERIALS:
One matboard 11x14"
Razor blade
#810 tape

1. Set the guide bar and stops to 2 1/2".

2. Place the mat in the cutter **face down** and cut three sides.

3. Raise the cutter bar to permit access to the cuts. Place tape directly on the three cuts.

4. Lower the bar and and cut the fourth side.

5. Remove the top and bottom stops. Leave the mat guide set at 2 1/2".

6. Place the mat **face up** in the cutter. Insert the blade partially into the board at the top of the existing cut—this method depends on hand control to keep from cutting all the way through the board **and** good vision to see the existing cuts. Follow the cut around the mat. A sliver of matboard surface paper will be released with each cut.

7. Clean up corners as necessary with a razor blade or X-Acto knife.

8. Set the guide and stops to 3" and cut a regular mat opening.

3-D DOUBLE BEVEL MAT

Open V-Groove Mat

MATERIALS:
Two 11x14" matboards (one White, one Gray)
Sheet of double-sided adhesive:
    Crescent's Perfect Mount Film or 3M's PMA
Squeegee

1. Cut a 3" border on the Gray mat and set aside. This will be the undermat.

2. Apply PMA to the back of the White matboard. Use a squeegee to create a good bond.

3. Place the White mat in the mat cutter **face down** and cut a 2 3/4" border. Discard the fallout.

4. Place the White mat back in the cutter **face up** and cut a 2 1/4" border. This creates the double-beveled piece. Set it aside.

Profile of a mat border with a 3-D double bevel

5. Place the White mat back into the cutter, **face down**, and cut a 2" border. There are now two pieces of White to adhere to the Gray mat. The fallouts can be used to help position them.

6. Peel the release paper from the back of the 2" White mat and adhere it to the Gray mat.

7. Peel the release paper from the back of the 1/2" double bevel piece and position it in the center.

The space between bevels can be adjusted to allow as much of the undermat color to show as desired.

APPLIQUE OR OVERLAY MAT

This mat uses two pieces of matboard of equal size. One becomes the solid undermat, the other is cut into one narrow double-beveled strip mat and attached to the surface of the undermat, serving as a dimensional decorative border.

MATERIALS:
Two matboards size 11x14"
    White for the undermat
    Gray for the overlay
Sheet of double-sided adhesive: Perfect Mount or PMA
Squeegee

1. Cut a 3" border on the White mat and set it aside.

2   Apply an adhesive sheet to the back of the Gray board. Squeegee to secure the adhesive bond. Leave the release paper on the adhesive until ready to place the decorative borders on the undermat.

3. Place the Gray board in the cutter **face up** and trim 1 3/4" from all four sides, creating a piece of beveled board 7 1/2x10 1/2".

4. Place the Gray board in the cutter **face down** and cut a 1/4" mat. Careful at the corners. This is the applique. Handle carefully, as narrow borders tend to bend.

5. Peel the release paper from the narrow overlay border. Position and adhere the border on the surface of the White mat, taking care to place them squarely. The fallout may be helpful in positioning the border.

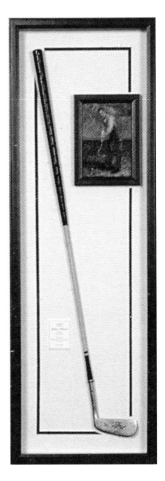

The shadow box framing of a golf club and painting is accented with an applique strip mat made from suede matboard.

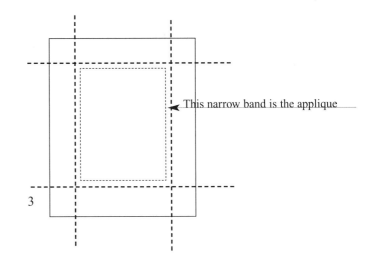

This narrow band is the applique

3

REVERSE BEVEL MAT

A mat cut with a reverse bevel has no visible bevel. This means the core of the board does not show, which is sometimes an advantage. Instead of descending toward the art as a beveled mat appears to do, a reverse bevel mat appears to float slightly above the surface of the art. Reverse bevels are often used when making fabric-covered mats.

MATERIALS:
One matboard, size 11x14"
Hard lead pencil
Vinyl eraser

FACE UP METHOD
1. Using a hard pencil, lightly mark a 3" border on the face of the mat.

2. Place the board in the mat cutter **face up** and cut all four sides. Do not overcut the corners at all.

3. Clean up the corners with a razor blade as needed. Gently erase the pencil lines with a vinyl eraser.

FACE DOWN METHOD
1. Using a pencil, mark a 3" border on the back of the matboard.

2. Remove the mat guide from the mat cutter to allow the matboard to extend beyond the left side of the cutter.

3. Place the board in the cutter **face down**, and slide the majority of the board to the left of the cutting head. Use the bottom mat guide to keep the board positioned squarely. Cut all four sides of the mat, always keeping the majority of the board to the left of the cutting head.

A double-reverse bevel mat is used to frame this puzzle. The reverse angle of the bevel helps to keep the puzzle in place.

FOIL MATBOARDS

Foil mats are cut from thin, foil-covered matboards, which are generally available in silver and gold. Because these boards scratch very easily, the are usually used as undermats or liners with other mats. Foil boards have a white core, which can be hidden if desired by cutting the mat with a reverse bevel. Burnish the opening for a finishing touch.

To cut the Gold Foil mat with a reverse bevel, set the guide and stops to 3"; insert the matboard **face up** in the cutter. Adjust the blade to a very short cutting depth.

Take great care not to extend the cuts at the corners, because this matboard is not deep enough to accommodate the usual type of cut.

Cutting 6- and 8-ply Mats

by Brian Wolf, CPF, GCF

The deep bevels of an 8-ply rag mat are dramatic, but many framers avoid them because they have a reputation of being a nightmare to cut. In reality, the techniques used to cut other matboards work just as well with thick matboards like 6- or 8-ply.

Adjust the blade as for any other board, so it cuts all the way through the 6- or 8-ply board and about a third of the way into the slip sheet. Use a standard .012 thickness blade, and use a fresh blade for each 8-ply mat opening. Although it may be possible to cut two or three openings without problems, why tempt fate with an expensive and challenging matboard?

Many framers fear that the extended blade can flex, creating a big risk of hooked corners. Although this is a valid concern, hooks are more likely to be caused by calibration problems or incorrect technique than by overextended blades.

Use a scrap of 6- or 8-ply board to calibrate the stops for perfect corners. Then cut the opening, slowly.

—or—

If you don't get a perfect mat, try cutting the mat using two swipes per cut. For the first cut, set the blade to a little less than normal depth. Set the stops to overcut at least 1/2" at the start of the cut and about 1/4" at the finish. This is crucial. The long front overcut provides a precise path for the second cut to track through; if there is a hook, it only affects the first 1/4" of the overcut.

Then reset the stops to the proper dimensions, and extend the blade to cut all the way through the 8-ply matboard.

Be very deliberate as you enter the board for the second cut. Make sure the blade enters the initial slice precisely to avoid seeing marks from the first cut on the bevel.

The Exit Scratch

Whether the mat is cut with one swipe or two, there is one detail that both methods share: the exit scratch. When any matboard is cut, the blade slightly scratches the bevel as it exits the board. A minor problem with standard thickness matboard, but in an 8-ply matboard it is obvious. Examine a mat you have cut. If you can see a scratch, try releasing pressure on the mat cutter handle and lifting it slightly before letting the blade lift out of the board.

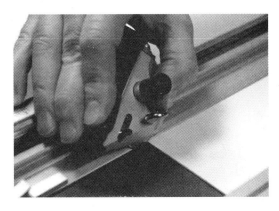

Adjust the blade so it cuts all the way through the 6- or 8-ply board and about a third of the way into the slip sheet.

CHAPTER 3

ANGLE CUTS

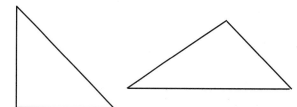

The use of angle attachments will increase efficiency when cutting these mats. Keencut, Fletcher and C&H have angle guide attachments. As an alternative to angle guide attachments, use geometry-style triangles which provide 45/90 and 30/60 degree angles.

DIAMOND MAT

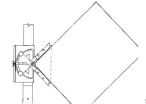

MATERIALS:
One matboard size 11x14"
Pencil and Rule

1. Measure and mark a 1 3/4" border on the back of the mat.

2. Measure and mark the center of each of the four borders.

3. Connect the four points, place the board **face down** in the cutter, and cut the four sides.

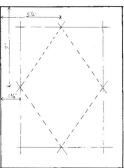

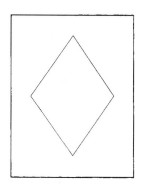

SIX-SIDED MAT

MATERIALS:
One matboard size 11x14"
Pencil and Rule

1. Measure and mark a 2" border on the back of the matboard.

2. Measure 5 1/2" from the edge of the matboard on all four sides and make marks that intersect the 2" marks.

3. Using a rule, connect the points to draw the six sides.

4. Place the board **face down** in the cutter and cut all six sides.

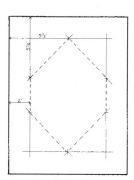

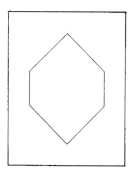

EIGHT-SIDED MAT

MATERIALS:
One 11x14" matboard
Pencil
Angle guide

1. Set mat guide to 3", place matboard in the cutter **face down** and mark the 3" border with pencil on all four sides.

2. Place the angle guide onto the mat cutter
    —or—use a triangle to mark the corner cuts.

3. Cut the four corners.

4. Reset the side mat guide to 3" and cut the 4 sides.

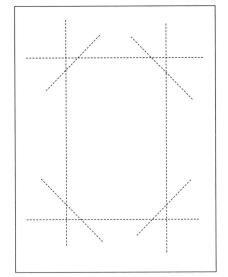

DOUBLE EIGHT-SIDED MAT

To make a Double Eight-Sided Mat, use the template double mat method (page 34).

1. Cut the 11x14" top mat. Save the fallout.

2. Trim the undermat to 10 3/4"x13 3/4".

3. Attach the undermat to the top mat with double-sided tape. Attach the fallout with double stick tape.

4. Set the side mat guide to 3 1/2". Use a pencil to mark the four sides.

5. Place the angle guide onto the mat cutter
    —or—use a triangle to mark the corner cuts.
    Cut the four angled corners of the undermat.

6. Reset the side mat guide to 3 1/2" and cut the four side borders.

Photo Corner Mat

Materials:
One matboard 11x14"
Angle guide
Pencil and Rule

1. Mark a 2" border on the back of the matboard.

2. Measure 4" from the outside of the matboard at eight points as illustrated. Connect the points with a rule.

3. Cut the four angled corners.

4. Cut the 2" border on all four sides, skipping the corners.

5. Set the mat guide to 2 1/2" and cut all four sides completely as with a typical mat.

Note: The size of the corner decoration is adjusted by changing the width of the border in step five. In the second illustration, the border size is 3".

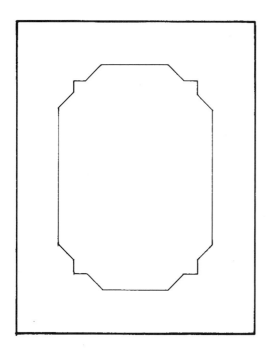

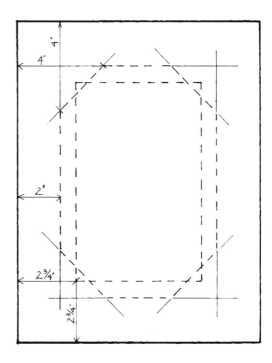

LATTICE CORNER

This mat is made using a 16x20" board instead of an 11x14" board because the complex latticework requires an expanse of space. A 4 1/4" border is used in this example. This design requires many short cuts—be sure to start and stop carefully. Although only a corner design is shown here, the lattice could also be extended to cover the entire mat if preferred.

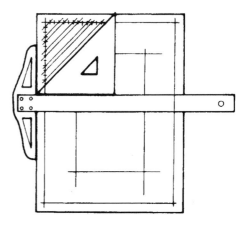

MATERIALS:
Two matboards size 16x20"
  White for top mat
  Use a color to show through the openings
T-Square
45-degree angle
Hard pencil

1. Place the White matboard **face down**. Measure and mark a 1" border along all four sides, then mark each 1/2" as illustrated.

2. Using a T-square and a 45-degree angle, draw the lattice design as shown. For clarity, it is helpful to lightly shade with pencil the squares that will be cut out and removed.

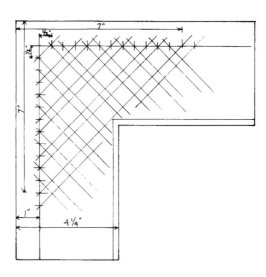

3. Remove the guide and stops. Insert the mat **face down** in the cutter. Align the cutter blade with one of the pencil lines and begin to make the short cuts. Throughout the cutting, it is important to make sure the bevels are cut in the correct direction, because the repeated bevel angle provides the shadow effect a real lattice would have.

4. Cut all the bevels in a line, then move to the next line. Make sure it is a line that should be beveled in the same direction as the previous cuts. Continue until all of the cuts with this bevel orientation have been completed on this corner.

5. Turn the board in the cutter and make all of the cuts on this side. Repeat on the other two sides.

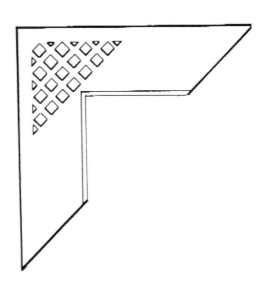

6. Some squares will fall out on their own, but many may not. To free the squares, work from the front with a new razor blade to finish cuts or clean up corners.

CHAPTER 4

OVAL & CIRCLE MATS

OVAL MATS

Oval mats must be cut with a machine that can correctly outline an ellipse. It is nearly impossible to cut a professional-looking oval mat by hand.

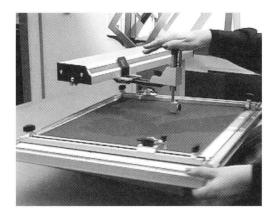

These directions use an overhead style oval cutter, which "hangs" over the matboard. The method described here can be used to cut ovals and circles of any size the machine is capable of making.

1. Position the trimmed matboard **face up** in the center of the cutter. Depending on the specific oval cutter, there are special rulers and other measuring devices that can be attached (if they are not already a part of the machine) that help to find the center and position the board.

2. Secure the matboard in the machine. Most machines use a clamping system with side hold bars to keep the board steady. With some models a couple of staples can be placed in the center of the board for extra security.

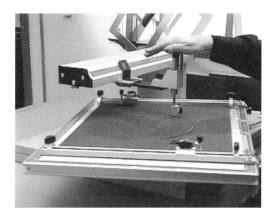

3. The settings for oval cutters are based on the difference between the height and width of the mat opening. For example, to cut an oval opening 8x10", the lower scale is set to 8", and the upper scale is set to 2"—the difference between 8" and 10".

4. Pull down on the top handle to lower the cutter onto the matboard.

5. Using two hands on the top knobs, start at 3 o'clock and, moving clockwise around the oval, apply even pressure. Some cutters cut all the way through the matboard on the first cycle, others work better if two passes are made.

6. When the matboard is cut cleanly all the way through, lift the top handle upward to release the cut matboard.

There are different knives available to cut at different angles, and also embossers that impress an accent line around oval and circle mat openings.

Portable Oval Cutters

Materials:
OvalArt mat cutter and accessories
T-square
Matboard
Pencil
3/4" plywood board 20x20"

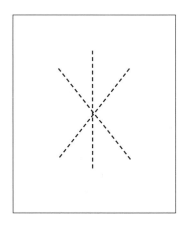

1. Use a T-square to locate the center of the face of the matboard. Draw lines to determine the exact center. This will serve as the positioning point for the metal plate.

1

2. Place the plate directly at the intersection of these lines, matching the marks on the plate to those drawn on the board. Nail to secure the plate.

3. Set the cutter to the proper opening and insert the cutting attachment into the center of the plate.

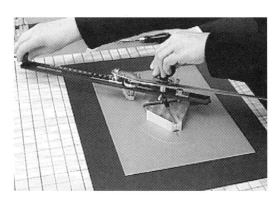

4. Position the blade at 9 o'clock. Applying even pressure, make one complete revolution.

5. Remove oval cutter attachment and remove plate.

Scalloper

The OvalArt Scalloper operates on the same principle as the OvalArt circle & oval cutter. Two to 32 scallops can be made by making multiple cuts.

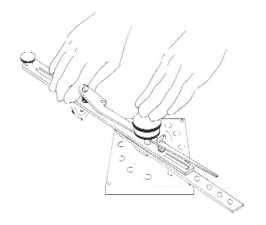

Oval Inlay

Materials:
Two matboards, size 11x14"
3M #810 tape

1. Cut both mats with an identical 8x10" opening.

2. Reset the cutter to cut a 9x11" opening and re-cut both mats. Save both 1" fallouts.

3. Attach the Gray inlay to the White mat, taping on the back with #810 tape.

Oval V-Groove

1. Insert the V-groove attachment into the oval cutter.

2. Increase the setting for the opening by 1/2" to 1" for placement of the V-groove on the mat.

3. Lower the V-groover onto the mat and rotate around the matboard, slicing through the cover paper only.

Embossed Ovals

1. Insert embossing attachment into the cutter.

2. Increase the opening measurement by 1/2" to 1", depending on desired placement of the embossed line.

3. Allow the embosser to drop onto the matboard. Press down and rotate to emboss the mat.

Adding Ink Lines

Several oval/circle cutters have attachments which allow ink lines to be added to a mat.

DOUBLE OVAL MAT

MATERIALS:
Two matboards, size 11x14"
    White top mat
    Gray undermat
Double-sided tape

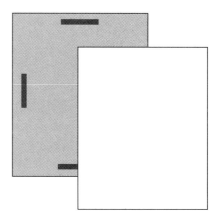

1. Apply double-sided tape to the face of the Gray matboard, along the outside edge. Attach the White mat **face up** on top of the Gray board.

2. Set the cutter for a 4 1/2 x 6 1/2" opening. Settings will be at 4 1/2" and 2". Center both boards beneath the cutter and cut an oval openings, cutting through the top board (White board) only. Remove the fallout.

3. Reset the cutter for a 4 3/4x6 3/4" (settings are 4 3/4" and 2") oval and cut the Gray oval.

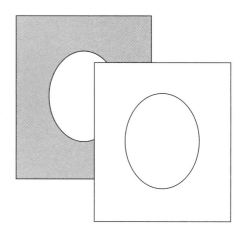

Note: As the blade cuts through the top mat, the tip will slightly scratch the undermat beneath it. This is virtually invisible on the finished double mat.

ROUNDED CORNER MAT

MATERIALS:
Oval mat cutter
Straight line mat cutter
One matboard, size 11x14"

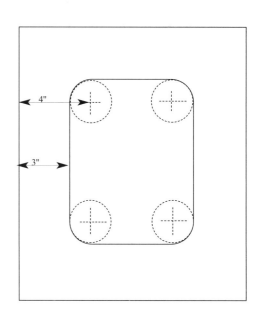

1. The circles will be cut first. Placement of circles: the width of the mat border plus the radius (1/2 of the diameter) of the circle locates the center point of each circle. In this example, that is 3" + 1", or 4". Mark the center points of the four circles. Cut the four circles.

2. Use the straight line cutter to cut the border on all four sides of the mat. Try to connect the straight lines to the circles very smoothly. Use an emery board to smooth any imperfect connections.

DOUBLE-OPENING OVAL MAT
For two 5x7 pictures

MATERIALS:
One matboard, size 11x14"

1. Layout the cutting plan using a pencil on the face of the matboard. Be careful not to mark outside of the area to be cut.

2. Set the cutter for a 4 1/2 x 6 1/2" oval opening.

3. Find the center of each mat opening Mark it on the board.

4. Place board in cutter **face up** with one of the centers positioned for cutting. Cut the oval.

5. Position the second center mark in the cutter and cut the oval. Be sure to maintain the same horizontal position or the ovals will not be level.

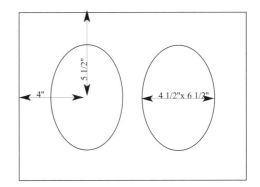

CIRCLE OPENING WITH A V-GROOVE ACCENT
The title block and a single rectangular mat completes this novel matting.

KOBE CORNERS

MATERIALS:
Straight line mat cutter
Oval mat cutter
One matboard, size 11x14"

1. Cut the circles first. The mat border will be 2" and each circle has a 1" radius. To measure the offset of the two circles at each corner, make a mark at 3" and 4" from both sides of each corner. Draw light pencil lines extending from each mark to the matching mark on the opposite end of the mat. The intersections where 3" lines cross 4" lines, and where 4" lines cross 3" lines— are the centers of the circles. Cut all eight circles using the oval cutter.

2. Cut a 2" border on all four sides with the straight line cutter.

3. Clean up any rough connections with an emery board.

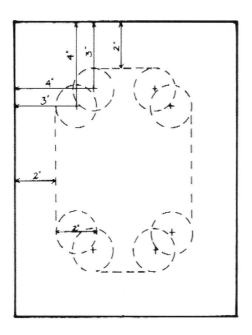

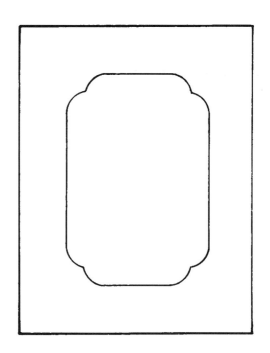

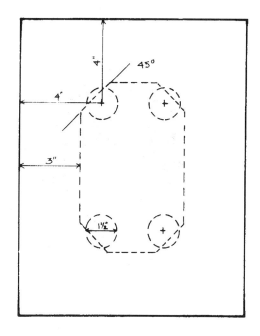

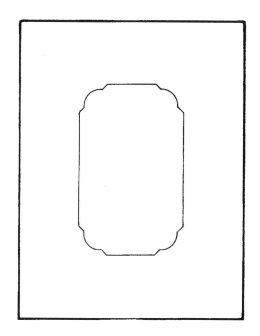

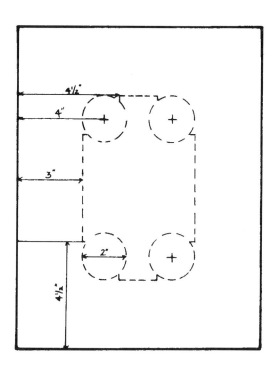

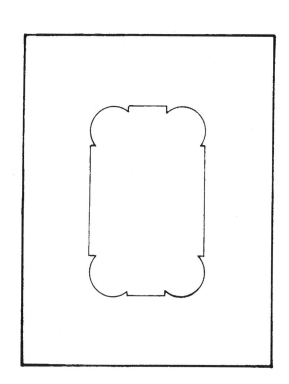

ARCH/ROMAN/GOTHIC MATS

Known by several names, the combination of rectangles with circles and ovals creates a mat opening with an old-fashioned, period character. There are several variations, but all of them consist of a rectangular cut on the bottom and sides of the mat, and a curved arch at the top.

Offset Arch with Circle Top

SIMPLE ARCH
MATERIALS:
Oval mat cutter
Straight line mat cutter
Matboard, size 11x14"

1. Measure 5 1/2" from the top and sides of the board. The intersection locates the center of the circle. Cut the circle.

2. Set the mat guide of the straight cutter to 2 1/2". Cut the bottom and side borders of the mat. Try to connect the straight lines to the curved top as smoothly as possible.

3. Smooth the connection points with an emery board if necessary.

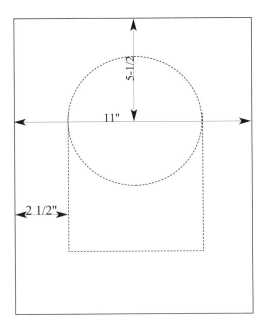

Arch/Roman/Gothic Mat Variations

These variations require a straight line mat cutter, an oval mat cutter, and one 11x14" matboard.

Offset Arch with Circular Top

Notched arches avoid the challenge of making a smooth connection between the straight lines and the curved lines.

1. Measure 4 1/2" down from the top of the board. Find the horizontal center of the board (5 1/2" from each side.) The intersection point locates the center of the circle.

5. Cut a 5" circle at that center point.

3. Place the board **face down** in the straight line mat cutter and cut a rectangular mat, with a 2 1/2" border on the sides and bottom, and a 4" border at the top.

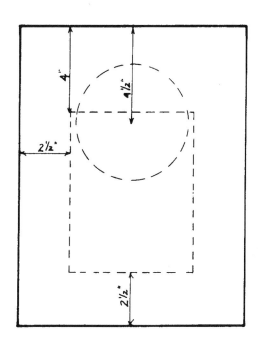

Offset Arch with Oval Top

1. Measure 5 1/2" from the top of the board. Find the horizontal center of the board (5 1/2" from each side.) The intersection marks the center of the oval.

2. Cut a 5 x 7" oval at this center point.

3. Place the board **face down** in the straight line mat cutter and cut a rectangular mat, with a 2 1/2" border at the bottom and sides, and a 4 1/4" border at the top.

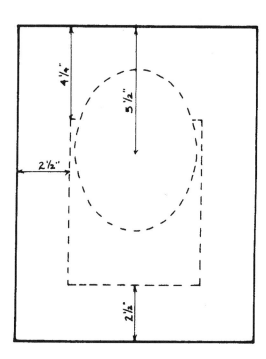

Combination Mat

MATERIALS:
Oval mat cutter
Straight line mat cutter
One matboard, size 11x13"

1. Find and mark the center of the face of the mat.

2. Set the oval cutter to cut a 6x8" oval.

3. Place the mat **face up** in the oval cutter and cut the oval. Tape the fallout back in place with removable tape #811.

4. Place the board **face down** in the straight cutter and cut a 3" border on all four sides.

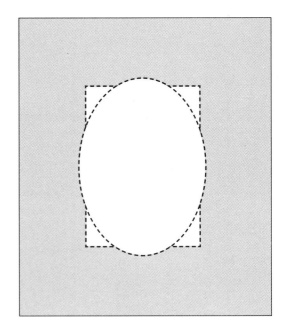

CHAPTER 5

SPECIAL CUTS

INSERTING FILLETS

MATERIALS:
11 x 14" matboard
3' of wood fillet
Double-sided tape
#810 tape
Corner Weld glue or Stapler and 3/16" staples

1. Cut a 2 1/2" border with a reverse bevel.

2. Miter one corner of the fillet using a chopper or fillet cutter, OR set a single-edged razor blade at a 45-degree angle on top of the fillet and use a hammer to force the blade through the wood.

3. Set the mat **face up**. Slide the fillet under the lip of the mat, with the mitered edge resting in a corner. Mark the position of the next miter on the fillet.

4. Cut the remaining three pieces of fillet using the process in step 3.

5. Apply double-sided tape to the flat area on the front of the fillet.

6. With the mat **face down**, place the four wood strips into the mat opening. Pay special attention to the corners, making sure the miters are aligned.

7. Once the four strips are securely in place, insert one staple across each corner or glue with Corner Weld.

8. Apply #810 tape to the back of the fillet to protect the artwork from the wood.

9. To make the back of the mat level with the protruding fillet, cut strips of matboard or foam center board and attach them to the back of the mat with double-sided tape.

mat
fillet
matboard filler

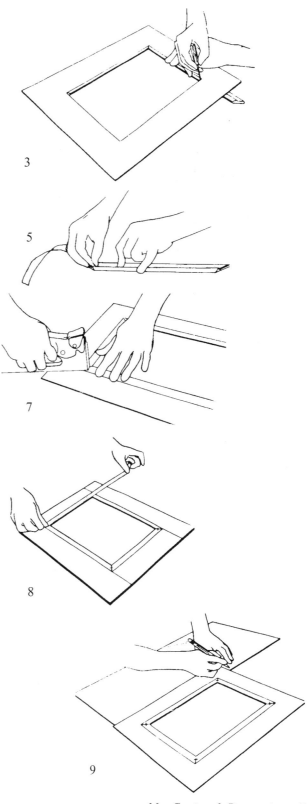

3

5

7

8

9

SINK MAT

A sink mat is useful when framing a thick object such as a book or magazine. This system fully supports the item in the mat without any hinges or tape.

MATERIALS:
Foam center board strips
Matboard for window mat
Matboard for backing

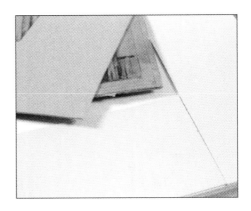

1. Determine Measurements.Center the book on the backing board. Measure the space from the edge of the book to the edge of the backing board. Cut strips of foam center board to completely fill the space on each side of the book, allowing no more than 1/8" of space between the strips and the book.

2. Layer strips of foam center board until they reach the same height as the book. Supplement the foam center board strips with a thinner piece of foam center board or strips of matboard if necessary to match the exact height of the book. Attach the layered strips to one another with glue or double-sided tape, and attach the stack to the backing board.

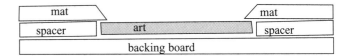

3. Measure the book. Cut a window mat 1/8" smaller than the book so the mat will slightly overlap.

4. Set the window mat on top of the stack(not the item!). The window mat may be attached to the stack with glue or tape. The package is ready to be placed in a frame.

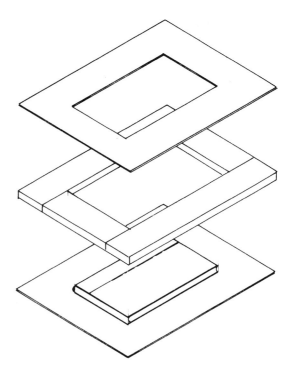

The Quick and Easy Shadow Box

This technique creates both the backing board and the lining for the sides of a shadow box—using one piece of board. Fabric-covered matboards, patterned-surface matboards, or fabric-covered foam center boards work the best, because the texture of these boards makes nearly-invisible corner seams. Matboard is strong enough for many items, but foam center board makes a sturdier unit, for larger or heavier objects.

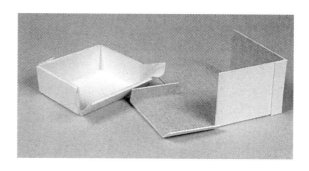

MATERIALS:
One sheet of matboard or foam center board, 13x16"
Utility knife
Linen tape

1. Cut board to 13x16". If using foam center board, apply fabric to the face of the board.

2. Place the board **face down** and score a 1" border on all four sides using a utility knife and rule. This will make a Quick Shadow Box that fits an 11x14" frame, and accommodates objects up to 3/4" thick. The extra 1/4" is for the glazing, and for space between the glazing and the objects.

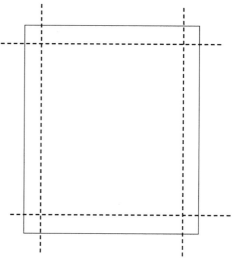

3. Cut out the four squares at the corners.

4. Place the board **face up**. Fold the ends upward and tape the outside of the four corners. Gummed paper tape works very well, because it does not stretch.

5. Items can be glued, sewn or otherwise attached to the Quick Shadow Box.

6. Select a frame of sufficient depth. Insert glazing, insert the Quick Shadow Box and fit as usual.

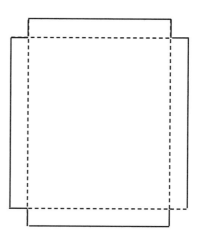

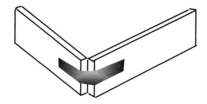

Securing the corners with gummed paper tape works very well, because it does not stretch.

COVE MAT

The cove mat has raised edges that slope downward to the artwork, drawing the viewer's eye to the art. Because its construction provides some depth, the cove mat can be useful for framing objects, but it is also an attractive, sophisticated border for art on paper.

Fabric-covered matboard works best, because the fibers tend to disguise the seams. If a custom-covered look is preferred, apply the fabric after the corners of the cove are joined for a seamless design. See page 85, Covered Mats, for the application procedure. Use a small brayer and gentle pressure to adhere the fabric to the corner seams.

MATERIALS:
12x15" matboard
     (outside dimension will be 11x14" when completed)
#810 tape or linen tape
Metal straight edge
Utility knife

1. Cut a typical 4" border on the matboard.

2. Set the guide to 3 1/2". Insert the matboard **face up** in the cutter and score (do not cut all the way through) all four sides. This will be the offset, which is necessary to the structure of the mat.

3. Using a metal straight edge and pencil, draw a pie-shaped wedge at each corner—the wider the wedge the deeper the cove; the smaller the wedge the smaller the cove. To make an 11x14" mat from the 12x15" matboard, the widest part of each wedge should be 1/2" wide.

4. Cut out the wedges with a utility knife and straight edge. Discard the wedges.

5. Join each corner with #810 or linen tape.

6. Using double-sided tape, attach a small piece of matboard to the rabbet of the frame in each corner, to support the cove.

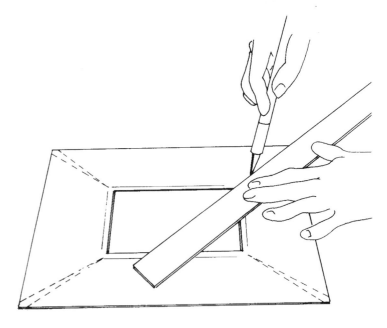

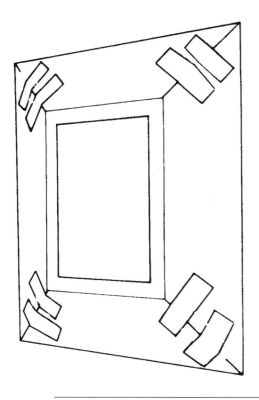

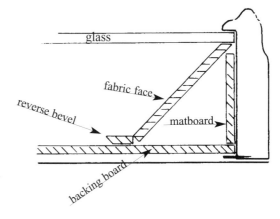

glass

fabric face

reverse bevel

matboard

backing board

SPACER MAT

This method provides space between the backing board and
the mats. It is useful when framing objects or floated
paper art, or for added dimension whenever it would visually enhance the framing design. Spacer mats can be layered to achieve whatever depth is needed.

MATERIALS:
Matboards
Foam board
Straight line mat cutter
Double-sided tape

1. Measure a border on the foam center board that is
   smaller than the width of the mat so that it will not be
   visible from the front of the frame. Use the regular mat
   |cutter with the blade extended.
   Cut out the window in the foam center board. It is
   okay if the corners are overcut; they will not show.
   Discard the fallout.

2 Cut the mat or mats.

3. Using double-sided tape, attach the foam board mat to
   the backing, then attach the mat to the foam center
   board.

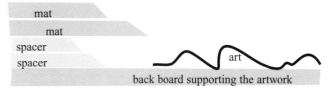

mat
mat
spacer
spacer
art
back board supporting the artwork

TITLE BLOCK
FOR A DUCK STAMP

MATERIALS:
White matboard size 13 3/4 x 14 1/2"

1. Mark back of board with pencil as illustrated.

2. Set the mat guide and stops to 3 1/8". Place the board in the cutter **face down**. Cut the sides and the top border.

3. Remove the stops and reset the mat guide to 1 3/4". Cut the bottom of the title block.

4. Reset guide to 4" and cut the bottom border of the mat.

5. Remove the guide and stops. Use the pencil lines to hand guide the last three cuts of the title block.

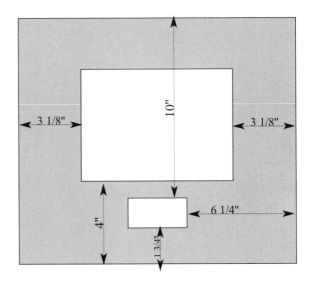

SCROLL MAT

This mat mimics the proportions of an oriental scroll. Use silk-covered or Oriental rice paper-covered matboards to enhance the oriental design.

MATERIALS:
Two matboards, size 10x24"
    White Silk top mat
    Tan Silk undermat
Pencil
T-Square
Double-sided tape or white glue

1. On the back of the White Silk matboard, mark a 2" border on the sides and a 5" border on the top and bottom. Cut mat as usual.

2. On the back of the Tan Silk matboard, mark a 2 1/2" border on the sides, and a 5 1/2" border on the top and bottom. Cut as usual.

3. Attach the mats together with double-sided tape or white glue.

The sides should be one third or less than the width of the top and bottom borders.

OVERSIZED MATBOARD

A 40x60" mat can be cut with a 40" cutter. The width of the mat border cannot exceed the distance from the bar to the hinge on the cutter.

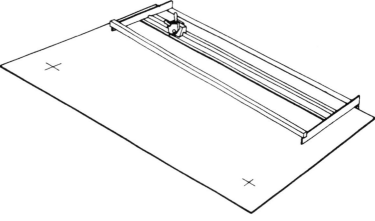

1. Trim the matboard to the outside dimensions. In this example, the entire 40x60" board is used, and the mat border will be 5", making a 30x50" opening.

2. Measure and mark the corner intersections of the mat border **on the face** of the board, using a hard pencil and a light touch.

3. Remove the stops and side mat guide from the cutter.

4. Insert the matboard **face up** in the cutter, with the majority of the board extending to the **left** of the cutting head as illustrated.

5. Slide the board until the pencil mark at the upper right corner of the board aligns with the cutting bar, positioned so the cutting head can reach the top of the cut.

6. Begin the cut at the top of the cutter and bring the cutting head down as far as possible. Let the blade lift out of the board.

7. Lift the cutting bar and slide the matboard upward along the cutter base until the bottom portion of the mat is within the range of the cutting head.

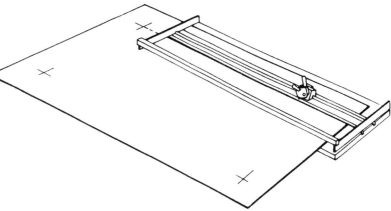

8. Resume the cut, taking care to position the blade directly on the same line as the previous cut. Cut until the blade reaches the bottom intersection of pencil lines— do not overcut.

9. Repeat the procedure on the other three sides.

10. Use an emery board to clean up the connecting cuts.

SPLICED MAT

This technique is used to make large mats—even huge mats. The example here will make a 54x78" mat with an 8" border. The splicing method uses two or three matboards. They may all be the same color, which makes the seams nearly invisible, or multiple colors may be used for a more dramatic design. Choose the color combinations as when designing any mat—the colors should complement the artwork and work well together.

MATERIALS:
Straight line mat cutter
Pencil
45-degree triangle
Three matboards
    two 40x60"
    one 32x40"
Another set of hands to help handle the large pieces!

THE INVISIBLE SPLICE METHOD

1. Trim the two 40x60" boards to 36x54".

2. Using a T-square and pencil, measure and mark an 8" border on both short sides and one long side of the back of the 54x36" boards.

3. Using the straight line mat cutter, cut the three marked sides of the mat opening on both large boards.

4. Trim the 32x40" board into two strips 10x30" each.

5. Set the mat guide to 2" and bevel one long edge of both 10x30" pieces, creating two 8x30" strips.

6. With a pencil, make two light marks 6" apart on the bevel edge of the strips, approximately in the center of the strip. Using a triangle, mark both sides of the angle splice on the two center strips—narrow end of the triangle towards the bevel, lined up with the 6" pencil marks. Cut a regular bevel all the way across the 8" strip, following the angle line.

7. On the face of one of the 36x54" mats, place the triangle with its long edge aligned with the innermost point of the "U". Mark the angle in pencil. Repeat on the other large mat. Cut a reverse bevel on all four lines. The bevels on the strips and the reverse bevels on the mats will fit into one another.

8. Place all of the pieces **face down** on the worktable and tape all of the seams with #810 or Lineco's Gummed paper tape which is very strong and does not stretch.

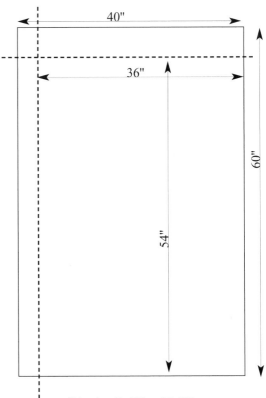

Trim the 40x60" to 36x54".
Make two of this size.

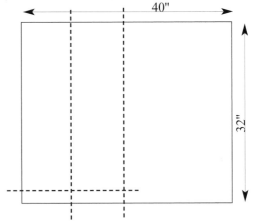

Trim two 10x30" pieces from a coordinating color matboard.

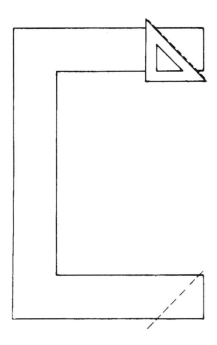

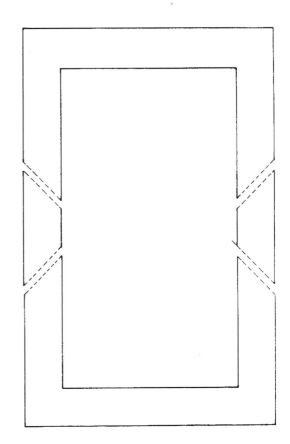

THE V-GROOVE METHOD

The previous method makes a nearly-invisible join between the board pieces. As an alternative, the join can be made a part of the design by creating a V-groove at each seam.

1. Follow steps 1-6 of the invisible splice method on the previous page.

2. Follow step 7, but make the marks on the back of the large mats. Place each three-sided mat in the cutter **face down** and make the angled cuts.

3. Place all of the pieces **face down** on the worktable and tape all of the seams with #810 or Lineco's Gummed paper tape which is very strong and does not stretch.

Note—if planning to cover the board with fabric, use overlapping bevels, paste them together with white glue and burnish them together. Then cover the boards with adhesive and apply the fabric.

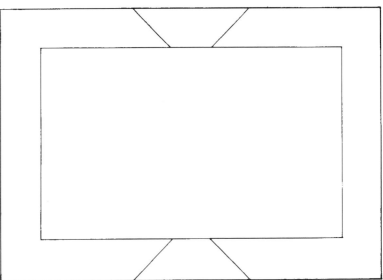

MULTIPLE OPENING MATS

This type of mat is popular for snap shots, photographs and memorabilia, which means the openings are often several different sizes. Layout may take longer than cutting. Save attractive layouts along with all of the measurements and calculations—there may be an opportunity to use them again.

MOM AND DAD
outside: 14x18"
openings: two 5x7"
v-groove accent

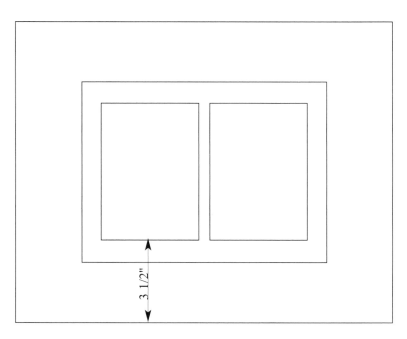

FOUR 35MM PHOTOS
outside: 11 x 14"
openings: four 3 x 4 1/2"

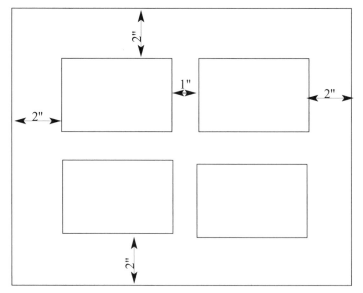

THE FAMILY GROUPING

outside: 16x20"
openings:
    two 4x6"
    four 3x3"
    two 2x 3"
    one 3x4"
    one Overlay Name Plaque 1x4

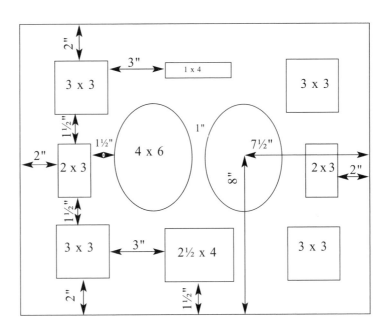

THE ANNIVERSARY MAT

outside: 16 x 20"
openings:
    one 4 1/2 x 6 1/2"
    four 3 x 4 1/2"
    three 2 x 3"
    four 1 1/2 x 2"

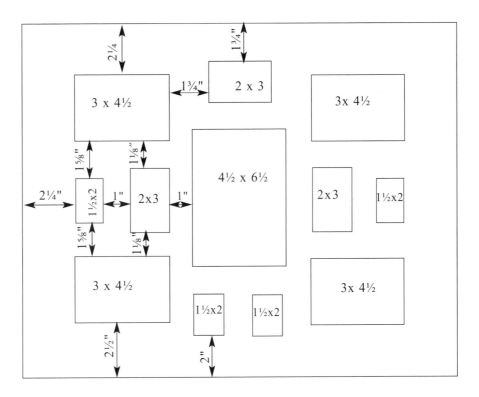

MOM AND DAD
outside: 11 x 14"
openings: two 5 x 7"
(41/2x61/2")

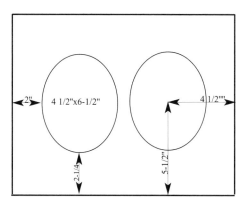

THREE OVALS
outside: 7 x 14"
openings: three 3 x 4"

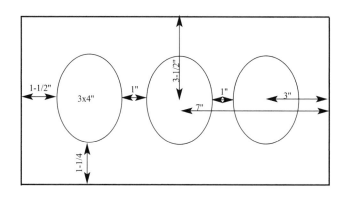

FIVE OVALS
outside: 11 x 14"
openings: five 3 x 3 1/2"

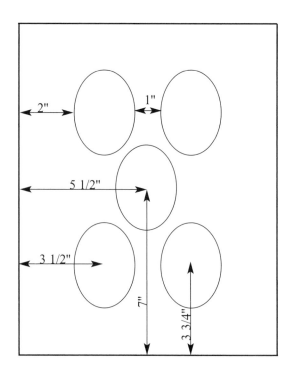

CHAPTER 6

MAT DECORATION

Beyond the many matting styles created with cutting methods, a wide variety of decorative techniques can be applied to the surface of the mat using inks, paints, tapes and other materials.

Just as with the cutting methods, decorative techniques can be subtle and unobtrusive or a dramatic artistic creation. This chapter will explore some of the most useful and popular surface decoration techniques.

MAKING A DECORATION BORDER GUIDE
This marking tool is handy when laying out decorative mats requiring parallel lines, and for indicating placement of designs. When this tool is used to lay out lines that will surround the mat opening, only the four corners are marked, avoiding the need to draw a complete line that would have to be erased later.

This type of guide can be purchased, or one can be easily made from matboard.

1. Cut the triangle and rectangle pictured, using a mat cutter, paper cutter or T-square and hand knife.

2. Glue the two pieces together.

3. Choose one of the rulers on this page and transfer the measurements to the guide, or make a photocopy and cut and paste it in place.

   A regular ruler does not work because it does not allow for the 45-degree angle of the corner. The rulers pictured here compensate for the angle.

The increments on these rulers have been calculated to produce the correct measurement when the guide is positioned in the corner of a mat opening.

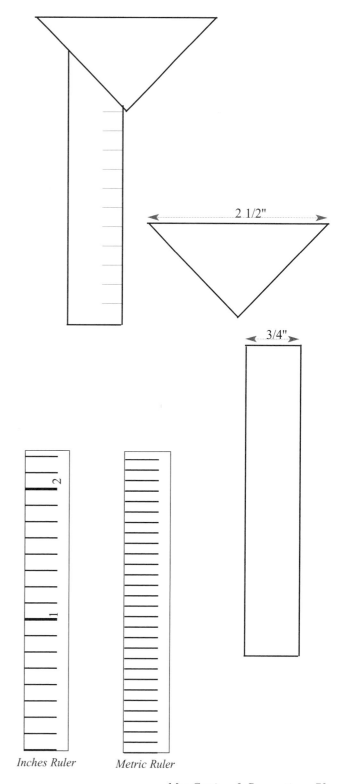

2 1/2"

3/4"

Inches Ruler　　*Metric Ruler*

INK LINES

Ruling pens are old fashioned graphic arts pens. These pens are used to draw draw decorative lines because they will hold almost any ink, watercolor or paint, including thick metallic paints.

A ruling pen consists of two blades, a center screw and a handle. The center screw can be adjusted to change the width between the blades which in turn determines the width of the ink line.

Ruling pens are available in different qualities. The better the pen, the smoother it will operate.

Thicker paints will require a wider blade setting.

Before filling the ruling pen with ink, draw several imaginary lines on a scrap of matboard to get used to holding the pen at the proper angle. If the pen has rough spots, carefully use an emery board to "sand" the edge smooth.

After filling the ruling pen with ink, practice many lines, both thick and thin until you feel comfortable with the pen.

Make sure the pen is working properly and the line is the proper width.

If the pen is sitting for a few minutes, the ink may dry. Dry ink will not allow the pen to function properly.

Keep both blades on the paper or matboard. They both must touch the board since the width of the blades determines the width of the line to be drawn.

Do not twist the pen while drawing the line; it will cause a skip in the line.

FILLING A RULING PEN
Always make sure to fill the pen away from the mat so the mat will not be damaged if the ink overflows from the pen while filling.

1. Set the blades to the desired width. The farther apart the blades, the wider the line.

2. Hold the pen at a slight angle or the ink will fall out.

3. Using an eyedropper, which may be on the inside of the cap of the ink bottle, or a brush, drop some ink between the blades.

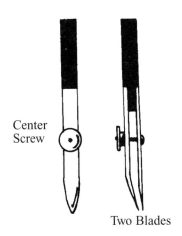

Center Screw

Two Blades

Use the pen at a slight angle — not straight up and down.

Make sure both blades touch the surface of the matboard.

Materials:
  11x14" mat with a 3 1/2" border
  ruling pen
  Permanent Artist's ink
  Decorative border guide
  Straightedge
  Pencil

1. Using decorative border guide, lightly measure desired
    lines from the bevel.

2. Line up straightedge with marks.

3. Fill ruling pen with ink and test on a piece of scrap
    board.

4. If more than one line is to be drawn, start with the one
    closest to the mat opening so that the next line may be
    started without waiting for the previous line to dry.

5. Set the ruler where line is to be drawn.

6. Place the tip of the pen at the exact starting point and
    draw the pen slowly along the straightedge ruler.

Note:
If the line is very long, the pen may run out of ink. Stop
before it runs out, refill the pen, test it on a scrap of
board, then set the pen **exactly next to** the end of the wet
line and continue drawing. The two lines will connect, if
they are both wet.

Take care not to move the ruler or the screw on the side of
the pen.

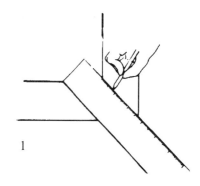

1

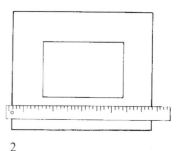

2

INK OVERRUN IN THE CORNERS?

Do not attempt to correct the overrun while the ink is wet
since this will result in a permanent smear.

Before the ink has time to cure, but after it is dry (generally
a few hours), slice the ink where the line should have ended
using a sharp razor blade.
  • Stand razor blade at the edge of the line, perpendicu-
    lar to mat, and *cut* the line then gently scrape the ink
    off.
  • Clean the board's surface with an eraser.

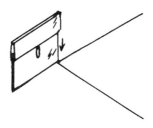

TRADITIONAL FRENCH MATTING

This classic decorating method consists of ink lines and watercolor wash panels.

MATERIALS:
Crescent Museum Solids Matboard
    The surface of this 100% cotton board is specially treated to accept paint and ink.
Artist Watercolor, transparent paint in small tubes.
Artist Permanent Ink.
2H to 4H (hard) pencil to mark line intersections.
Ruling Pen
    This old style mechanical pen can carry any type of liquid, thick or thin. It is adjustable for any line width.
Inking ruler
    Usually metal with a cork or fiber underside that keeps the ruler above the mat, allowing the ruling pen to run along its edge without smearing the ink.
Border Guide (page 73)
Soft watercolor brush, 1/2" to 3/4" flat
Mixing cup for watercolor.

To practice, cut strips of matboard 3x12". Fill the ruling pen with ink as shown. Draw 1/2"-wide panels using the ruling pen and ink. Practice making thin lines and thick lines by adjusting the knurl screw on the pen. Allow approximately 10 minutes to dry. Practice the watercolor technique, filling the panels with pale color.

MAKING A FRENCH MAT:

1. Cut the mat opening.

2. Place the border guide in one corner of the mat opening. Make a dot with a pencil at 1/8", 1/4", and 3/4". This will make a 1/2"-wide panel with an accent line 3/8" from the mat opening. Repeat the marking process in the other three corners.

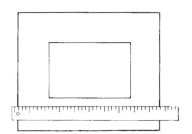

3. Practice drawing ink lines on scrap board until the desired width is achieved.

4. Fill the ruling pen with ink. Start with the line closest to the bevel. Place the tip of the ruling pen on the dot at the left and draw a continuous line to the dot at the right (opposite for left-handers). The drawing action of the pen should feel smooth. Do not press hard or the pen will pick up paper fibers causing spattering of the ink. Draw each line with a continuous stroke. Draw all three lines on one side, then do the opposite side. Let both sides dry. Do the remaining two sides. Let dry.

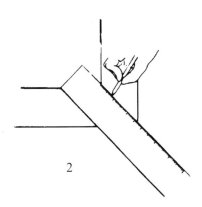

2

5. Place a dab of the color into a cup and mix with water. Test the color on matboard. It should be pale and transparent—French matting is a subtle technique.

6. Before applying watercolor to the mat, use the brush to apply a wash of clear water to the panel area. This permits the watercolor to be absorbed evenly, and makes it easier to correct errant brushstrokes.

7. Dip the brush into the watercolor. It should be wet but not dripping. Start 1" away from any corner. Rest the brush lightly on the matboard and pull the puddle of watercolor around the panel. Keep adding more watercolor as you go along. Do not let the puddle dry up. As you approach the last corner, lift the brush and wipe it on a paper towel to reduce the amount of color carried around the last corner. Blend the start and finish.

PROBLEMS?
Ink line extends beyond intersection?
Let it dry, then cut it with a razor blade and scrape off the excess ink.

Miss a spot?
Apply more color with the brush and blend. Pick up excess paint with the brush and wipe on a paper towel.

Overwash the panel lines?
Using a brush filled with clean water, scrub the overwash, wipe the brush on a paper towel, and repeat the process until the overwash is gone.

If you try to pick up the color with a paper towel an imprint of the towel will be left on the board.

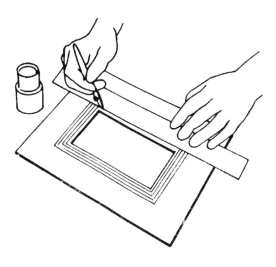

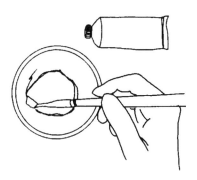

FRENCH POWDER PANEL

This technique uses artist pastels to simulate the look of a watercolor wash. Soft pastels (also called chalk pastels) are available in many colors from art supply stores. Use each color alone, or blend two or three together for customized colors. A bit of rottenstone can be blended with the powder to soften the intensity of strong colors.

MATERIALS:
Artist's soft (chalk) pastels
Permanent ink
Border guide (see page 73)
Ruler
White vinyl eraser
Hard pencil
Razor blade
Two poly foam brushes

1. Cut the mat. Decide where the decorative panel will be positioned, then mark the corners of the mat with dots using a pencil and the border guide or a ruler.

2. Fill the ruling pen with liquid acrylic paint or permanent ink.

3. Line up the rule with the dots closest to the bevel. Draw the line. Draw the next line parallel to the first. Continue working outward until all lines are drawn on one side of the mat. This method allows each new line to dry undisturbed while working on the others. Let them dry thoroughly. If there is an overrun, use a razor blade to cut and scrape off the excess.

4. Scrape a stick of soft pastel with a razor blade to create colored powder. Prepare all of the colors needed for the mat. These can be kept in small plastic containers; film case work very well.

5. Apply the powder to the panel with a poly foam brush. Cut the brush to a smaller size if necessary. Rub the powder gently onto the board—do not scrub.

6. Work the powder around the inside edge of the panel, all the way around the mat. Then apply powder to the outer edge of the panel and blend towards the middle.

7. Remove excess powder with a clean poly foam brush.

8. Use a white vinyl eraser to clean up stray powder.

Scrape a stick of soft pastel with a razor blade to create colored powder. These can be kept in small plastic containers; film case work very well.

A stencil can be made using 811 tape. It is available in a 2" wide width and can be applied to the edges of the ink ruled areas to keep the powder from straying over the edge of the panel.

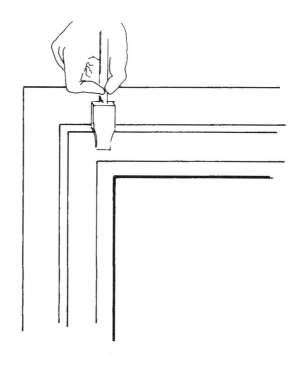

Work the powder around the inside edge of the panel, all the way around the mat. Then apply powder to the outer edge of the panel and blend towards the middle.

STENCIL DECORATION

Stenciling can be used to add a decorative accent that echoes a feature in the artwork.

MATERIALS:
Acrylic paints
Stencil brush or scrap fabric
Scrap of glass, Mylar or acetate
Removable tape (#811)
X-Acto knife, a design

1. Make a stencil of the design using a clear acetate or Mylar. Trace then cut out the design with an X-Acto knife. Be careful not to overcut.

2. Hold the completed stencil in position with 811 tape.

3. Squeeze acrylic paint onto a scrap of glass. Use a sponge brush or scrap of fabric to apply the paint -- practice first!

4. Carefully lift the stencil and let the paint dry.

PAINTED BEVELS

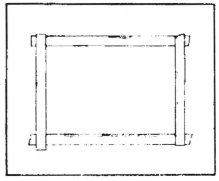

MATERIALS:
Matboard
Acrylic paints
Short bristle brush
3M #811 tape, removable type

1. Before cutting the mat, place four strips of #811 tape on the **face** of the mat in the area where the mat will be cut. Burnish lightly.

2. Place the mat **face down** in the cutter and cut a 3" border as usual. Discard the fallout.

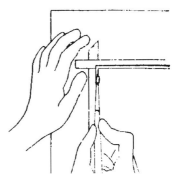

3. Set the mat on a scrap board **face up** and color the bevels with paint. Make the strokes downward, from the top of the mat down the bevel.

4. When dry, slowly remove the tape.

HAND CUTS

Each line of the design will require two cuts that face each other, to form a handmade V-groove.

MATERIALS:
Matboard
Flexible Rule or French Curves for drawing curves
Ruler
Tracing Paper
Soft and Hard pencil
X-Acto Knife

1. Trace the chosen design and transfer to the matboard by rubbing pencil on the back of the tracing paper and retracing onto the matboard.

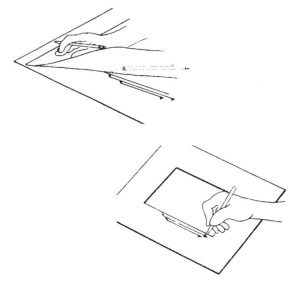

2. Using a pencil-style X-Acto knife and a rule as a guide, cut into the face of the board without going all the way through. Hold the knife at a 45 degree angle to make an open cut.

3. Turn the board around and slice all of the lines in the opposite direction of the first cuts.

4. Carefully remove the cut-out pieces from the design. Use the tip of the X-Acto knife to release any pieces still attached to the board.

TAPE LINES & MONOGRAMS

CHARTING TAPE MONOGRAM
MATERIALS:
11 x14" mat with 3" border
1/64" charting tape (from an art supply store)
Sheet of 1/4" transfer alphabet
Decorative border guide or T-square
Razor blade or X-Acto Knife
Burnisher
Pencil

1. Using a pencil and a T-square or the Decorative border guide, mark the desired position of the tape on the front of the mat.

2. Set the tape onto the face of the mat, being careful not to stretch it. Pat it down. Continue on the other three sides. Allow the tape to intersect and overlap at the corners.

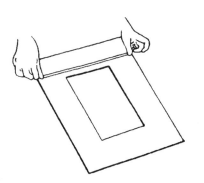

3. Use a razor blade or an X-Acto knife to miter the tape at the corners.

4. Lift off the loose ends.

5. If necessary, use a blade point to align the corners. Pat to adhere.

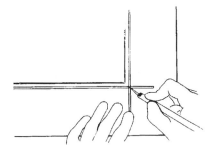

6. Determine the placement of the monogram. Cut away a section of the charting tape in that area. Place the alphabet transfer sheet on the mat, with the first appropriate letter positioned at the beginning of the empty area. Use a burnisher to rub the letter, transferring it onto the mat. Repeat the process with the remaining letter or letters.

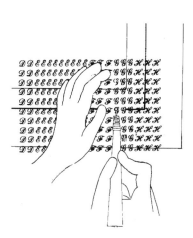

MARBLED PAPERS

Decorative papers can be used as panels or thin lines on the surface of a mat, or as a wrapping for thick or thin bevels. A variety of papers can be used, from handmade marbled paper to thin wallpaper to quality wrapping paper. If the mat will be used in conservation framing, be sure the decorative paper is acid-free.

The method shown here uses marbled paper that comes with an adhesive backing. If a decorative paper has no adhesive, mount it to a sheet adhesive such as Crescent's Perfect Mount Film before cutting into strips.

MATERIALS:
Border guide and pencil
Sheet of marbled paper
Perfect Mount film
X-Acto knife
45-degree triangle
Four small squares of release paper

1. Cut an 11x14" mat with a 3" border.

2. Using a hard pencil and border guide, mark the areas where the paper panels will be placed.

3. Place the paper in the straight line mat cutter **face up**. Use the right hand side of the bar as a guide. Use a razor blade to slice the strips to the desired width.

4. Place the four pieces of release paper in the four corners to keep the tapes from adhering before you are ready for final placement.

5. Peel the backing off one of the strips and carefully place it on the marked area. Let the tape rest on the release paper in the corner. Set the remaining strips in place.

6. Place a piece of release paper between the overlapping tapes to prevent the two strips from sticking to one another. Line up a rule or 45-degree angle at each intersection and slice through both pieces of paper with an X-Acto knife. Slice through both strips in one stroke.

7. Remove all of the release paper and excess tape. Press the tape to adhere at the corners, making sure the miters meet properly.

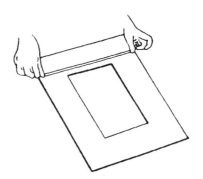

Marbled papers are available in a wide variety of color combinations and patterns.

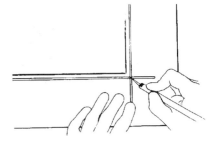

PAPER FILLET

MATERIALS:
11x14" matboard
3M #810 tape
A Decorative Paper such as:
  Marbled paper
  Thin wallpaper
  Quality wrapping paper

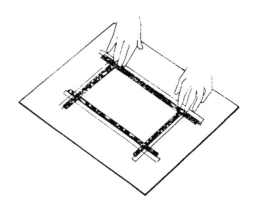

1. Cut an 11x14" mat with a 3" border.

2. Cut two 1x7" pieces and two 1x10" pieces from the decorative paper.

3. Fold the four pieces horizontally.

4. Place the mat **face down** and set a strip of folded paper along the mat opening, allowing the paper to extend 1/4" into the opening. Secure the strip with #810 tape.

5. Apply the remaining three strips in the same way, checking to make sure all of the strips extend into the opening the same amount. The overlapped corners will look fine if the paper is patterned.

LACE FILLET

1. Cut the mat to desired size. Allow for the width of the lace to lay over the photo.

2. Set the mat **face down** on the worktable and apply the strips of lace. The lace may be taped into position with 810 tape, pressure-sensitive linen tape or glued with white glue onto the back of the mat.

Corner may overlap or be mitered, depending on the lace.

GLASS MAT

With the use of a sheet of masking and spray paint, a sheet of glass can become a glossy mat border. Use a spacer mat hidden beneath the glass to protect the art from the paint and to provide airspace in the frame.

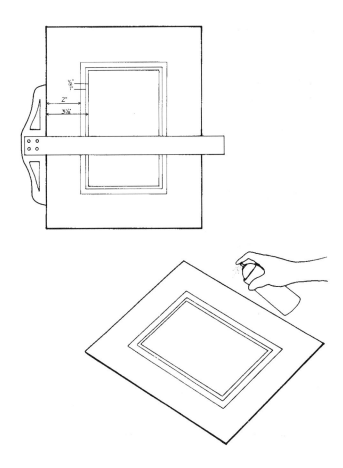

MATERIALS:
1 lite of regular glass, 11x14"
Clear contact paper
Hand-held squeegee
Single-edged razor blade or X-acto knife
Ruled T-square
Spray enamel, matte finish (or satin)

1. Clean the glass thoroughly on both sides

2. Apply a layer of clear contact paper to the entire lite of glass. Use a squeegee to burnish the contact paper. Work air bubbles from the center outward.

3. Trim excess contact paper from the edges.

4. Measure and mark the borders with a T-square, using the measurements in the diagram.

5. Using a knife or blade, carefully cut on the lines. Do not overcut.

6. Peel off A and C. Check all edges for tightness, and burnish any area of the contact paper that has lifted from the glass.

7. Spray entire glass with paint—use 3 or 4 light coats. If the layers are too heavy, the paint will lift.

8. Set aside to dry.

9. Peel off B and D. If paint oozed under the contact paper, clean it off with a razor blade. Be very careful.

Note: To make an oval, use an oval mat cutter with the plastic scoring tool attachment to measure and cut the contact paper in steps 4 and 5.

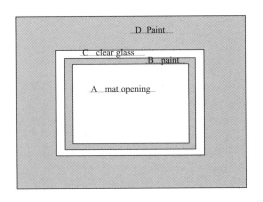

CHAPTER 7

FABRIC-COVERED MATS

FABRIC-COVERED MATS

Fabric-covered mats offer texture and richness of color. Although many fabric-covered matboards are available from manufacturers, fabric-wrapped bevels and mats covered with a customer's fabric are important skills to offer. Use opaque fabrics such as cotton, velvet, linen, or silk.

Lay the fabric on the board to see how the board color will influence the overall appearance of the mat. Sheer and loose-weave fabrics are especially affected by the underlying board color.

Several methods can be used to attach the fabric to the matboard. Following are directions for dry/heat, wet, and cold pressure-sensitive mounting.

DRY MOUNTING

MATERIALS:
11x14" mat with a 3" border, reverse bevel
Release paper, Fusion 4000
X-Acto knife
Fabric
Heat press, mechanical or vacuum
Tacking iron

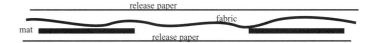

1. Cut a piece of mounting tissue 11x14". Align the tissue with the edges of the mat. Tack the tissue, in one spot, to the face of mat.

2. Tack the fabric to the tissue in one spot. Use release paper between the tacking iron and the fabric.

3. Place the mat/tissue/fabric stack between two pieces of release paper.

4. Place the stack of materials in the press. Dwell time (time in the press) depends on the type of adhesive tissue and the thickness of the fabric.

5. Remove from the press. If the fabric is very thick or stubborn, put it under weights while it cools.

6. Place the mat **face down** and slice the fabric in the window opening, being careful not to overcut in the corners.

7. Fold each of the four flaps around the bevel and tack to the underside of the mat. Place in the press to bond. Use the tacking iron to finish edges and corners if necessary.

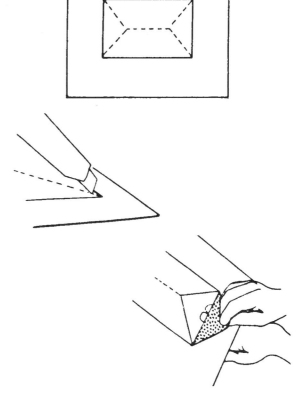

WET MOUNTING

MATERIALS:
11x14" mat, 3" border with reverse bevel
Mounting paste
Brush
Fabric

1. Using a brush or roller, apply mounting paste to the front of the mat.

2. Lay the fabric on the wet paste. Be sure the grain of the fabric (the woven threads) is parallel to the edges of the mat. There is no excuse for wavy lines or crooked fabric.

3. Place the mat fabric side down and cut out a window in the opening. Slice toward each corner, careful to stop just short of the mat corner.

4. Apply mounting paste to the sliced flaps of fabric. Wrap the four sections to the underside of the mat. Watch for excess paste in the corners—wipe it up right away. A small pointed tool may be useful to make a tight fit.

5. Apply pressure to create the bond. A dry mount press or a vacuum press may be used (it will remove moisture as well as apply pressure), or place the mat under a lite of glass or other weight and allow to dry.

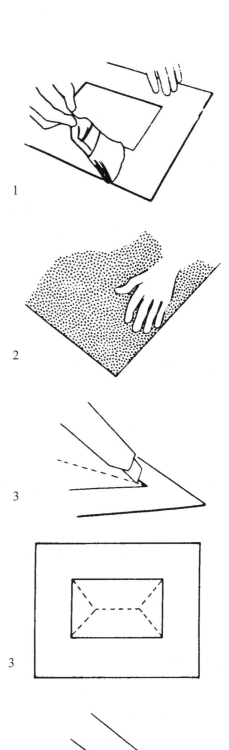

COLD MOUNTING

MATERIALS:
11 x 14" mat, 3" border with reverse bevel
one sheet Perfect Mount Film or 3M's PMA
Squeegee or Cold Mount Press
Fabric

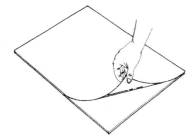

1. Apply adhesive sheet to the back of the fabric. Squeegee to bond.

2. Peel the release sheet from the adhesive then apply the fabric to the face of the mat. Line up the fabric weave. Squeegee to bond.

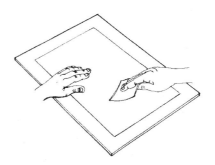

3. Place fabric-covered mat **face down** and cut out the window—be careful of the corners.

4. Wrap the fabric flaps over the bevel and press to secure.

5. Use a squeegee or cold mount press to create the overall bond.

SPRAY MOUNTING

   Spray glues, no matter how permanent they purport to be will not hold up for the purposes of professional picture framing.
   Buckling and bubbles are often the problem once the weather changes. Over time the adhesive dries out, discolors and leaves the fabric loose and stained.

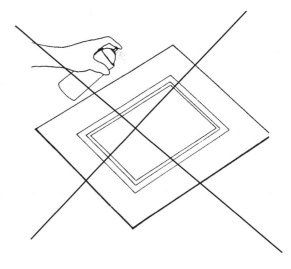

FABRIC-COVERED DOUBLE MAT

By stacking two mats and covering the entire unit with fabric, a subtle but distinctive dimensional effect is created.

MATERIALS:
Cut one mat with a 4" border
    one with a 3 1/2" border, Save the fallouts.
Linen or other opaque woven fabric
Mounting paste such as YES paste, SOBO or Lineco NpH.
Lite of glass

WET PASTE METHOD

1. Set the bottom mat **face up** on a sheet of release paper Apply wet paste to the surface of the mat.

2. Place the top mat onto the wet surface of the undermat. Apply wet paste to the surface of the top mat be sure to cover all bevels and layers.

3. Place the fabric over the wet pasted mats. Be sure to align the weave of the fabric with the mats—keep it parallel.

4. Gently replace the two fallouts (one at a time) coaxing the fabric into the corners of the mats. Watch out for wrinkles in the corners.

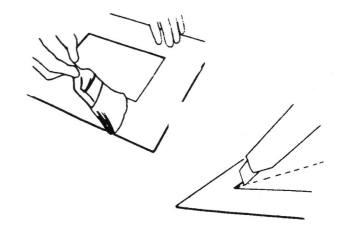

5. Remove any paste that may have squeezed out. Set a lite of glass with a weight on top, or place in a vacuum press or mechanical dry mount press to dry and bond.

6. When dry, remove from beneath glass or from press. Place the mats **face down**, keeping the fallouts in place.

7. Slice a window opening in the fabric. Be careful in the corners. Wrap the flaps around to the back of the mat. Adhere with wet paste. tidy up the corners. Allow to dry.

DRY MOUNT METHOD

1. Cut the mats.

2. Place a sheet of Fusion 4000 between and on top of the doublemat stack.

3. Place the mats with the adhesive between two pieces of release paper.

4. Set a piece of sponge over the top of the release paper. This will force the fabric and the Fusion into the beveled openings.

The fallouts from the mats may be useful to force the fabric and adhesive into the openings --it depends on the thickness and the stretch of the fabric. Experiment.

Once mounted, ste the double mat face down and slice a window opening in the fabric. Be careful in the corners. Wrap the flaps around to the back of the mat.   Adhere with the tacking iron.

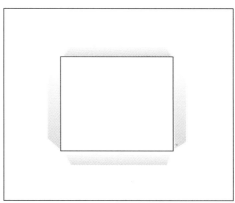

sponge pad
release paper
Fusion 4000
mat   Fusion 4000
mat
release paper

Wrapped Deep Bevels

Materials:
Matboard color coordinated with the paper or tape used for wrapping the bevel edge.
Four strips of Mighty Core foam board
Paper or decorative tape to wrap the bevel
  Pressure-sensitive marble papers cut into tape width
  or pressure-sensitive linen tape for a white finish
810 tape
Double-sided tape
Perfect Mount Film double sided adhesive can be applied to the back of decorative papers.

1. Extend the blade on the straight line mat cutter to cut through foam board.

2. Bevel one edge of each of the strips of foam board.

3. Use a chopper or use a 45-degree angle and an X-Acto knife to miter both ends of each strip.

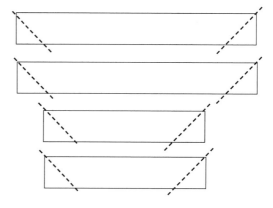

4. Choose the decorative wrap and cover the edge of the foam board. Take care not to get ripples or waves.

5. Lay the four wrapped strips face down and attach them to one another at the corners with 810 tape or gummed paper tape.

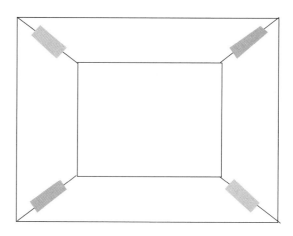

LACE/NET COVERED MAT

A sheer fabric, lace, or net fabric overlay makes an attractive accent mat for photographs, needlework, and vintage objects. The color of the underlying matboard is important, because it will show through the fabric.

MATERIALS:
11x14" matboard, with 3" border, reverse bevel
13x17" netting or shear fabric
Double-sided tape
Straight pins
Small roller

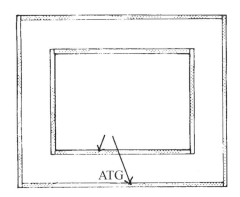

1. Place the mat **face down**. Apply strips of double-sided tape along the very edge of the mat opening. Then apply double-sided tape to the outer edges of the mat. Leave the backing paper on the tape.

2. Place the netting **face down** on a clean work table.

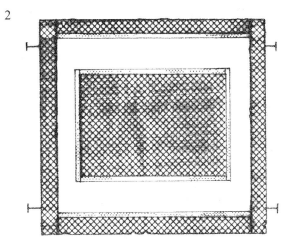

2

3. Set the mat **face down** on the net. Line up the pattern or woven lines very carefully. Secure with a few straight pins stuck into the core of the matboard.

4. Peel the backing paper from the tape at the outer edges of the mat. Lightly press the net onto the exposed tape. Do the four corners first, then work to the middle of each side.

4

5. Use a razor blade to cut out the center of the net, leaving 1" to wrap around to the back of the mat.

6. Peel the paper from the taper near the mat opening. Wrap the net to the back of the mat. Attach it lightly to the tape. Be careful in the corners.

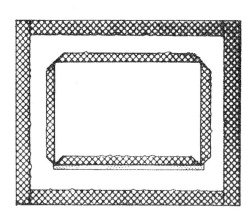

7. Reposition netting by lifting it from the tape and resetting it until satisfied with the placement.

8

8. Secure the netting by pushing a small roller over the taped areas.

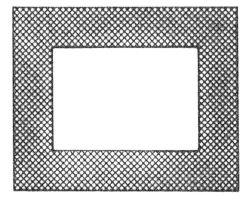

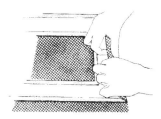

6

Wrapping the Bevel of a Fabric-Covered Matboard

This technique combines the convenience of purchased fabric-covered matboard with the custom refinement of fabric-wrapped bevels.

MATERIALS:
11x14" fabric-covered matboard
Double-sided tape or glue
Razor blade

1. Cut a 4" mat border and save the fallout.

2. Adjust the blade depth to cut through just the matboard—not the fabric. Use the fallout to practice making cuts that will cut the board but not the fabric.

3. Put the mat back in the cutter and cut a 3" border, once again cutting just through the board, not through the fabric.

4. Carefully peel the loose panel of matboard away from the fabric.

5. Apply double-sided tape to the underside of the mat very close to the bevel.

6. Slice the corners of the loose fabric with a razor blade, careful not to cut too far.

7. Wrap the loose fabric around the bevel and press onto the exposed tape. The corners may require special attention.

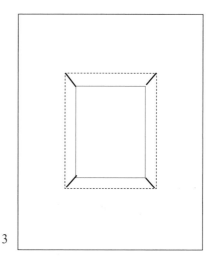

3

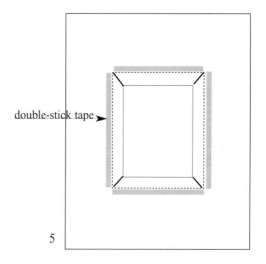

double-stick tape ▶

5

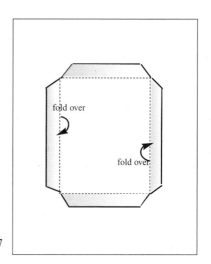

fold over

fold over

7

Woven Ribbon Mat

Materials:
Raffia or ribbon
Circle paper punch
11x14" matboards
    one dark
    one light
3M #810 tape

1. Cut a double mat. Carefully separate the two mats. Measure the top mat for placement of holes for weaving of the ribbon.

2. Use a common paper punch. Punch holes in the planned places and save the fallout circles—they will be needed. If making the punch is difficult, use a hammer and tap lightly on the top of the paper punch. This will help cut through the board.

3. Start anywhere from the back and weave the satin ribbon in and out of the matboard.

4. Set the mat **face down** and replace the circles that fell out of the holes. This gives a rounded smooth effect where the ribbon comes out of the holes.

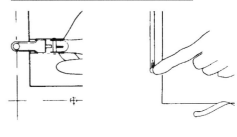

5. When the ribbon is correctly positioned, secure the back side with strips of 810 tape. Attach the undermat.

6. Attach bow separately. Be careful not to make the bow too thick or a shadow box will be required.

Threaded Lines

This method creates a quick and easy decorative line around the mat opening. A variety of threads and strings may be used to achieve many different effects. Gold metallic threads provide a gold line without the mess of inks.

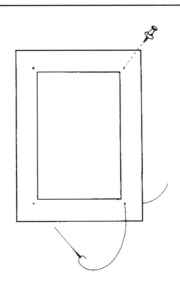

Mark placement on front of mat and poke holes with a needle or pushpin. The hole should be just large enough for the selected thread.

For a continuous line around the mat opening: Make one hole at each corner. Use four separate lengths of selected thread, several inches longer than needed for each side, threaded through a needle. Come up through one hole, and go down through the next, then tape or tie threads at back of mat. Repeat on all four sides of mat.

PADDED MAT

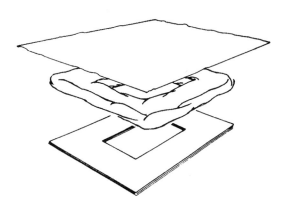

MATERIALS:
Two 11x14" White matboards
Sheet of polyester batting (from sewing shops)
Double-sided tape
Opaque woven fabric
Straight pins or push pins
Stapler and 3/16" staples

1. Cut a 3" border on both 11x14" matboards.
    Adhere the mats together, back to back, using white
    glue or double-sided tape.

2. Cut a piece of polyester batting 11x14".
    Set the batting on top of the mats. Using a scissors, cut
    an opening in the middle of the batting to match the
    mat opening as closely as possible.

5. Set the fabric on top of the padding and mats.
    Stretch the fabric over the outer edges of the mat and
    hold it in place with a few pins pushed into the edge of
    the matboard. Start in the four corners and work
    around, carefully matching the grain of the fabric to the
    edge of the matboard.

6. Use the stapler to fasten the fabric securely to the back
    of the mat, then remove the pins.

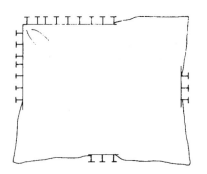

fabric

mat bevels

7. Cut an X in the center of the fabric, being careful to
    control the cut—do not exceed the mat opening.

8. Pull the flaps of fabric through the mat opening to the
    back of the mat. Adjust the grain of the fabric and the
    padding as needed and pin to the bevel of the mat.
    Work around the opening until everything looks even,
    then staple on the back side and remove the pins.

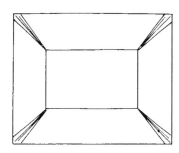

CORNER SUGGESTIONS

There are several ways to add interest to the corners of a
padded mat. Wrap grosgrain, satin or velvet ribbon diago-
nally over each corner and fasten to the underside of the
mat. Upholstery braid also works nicely.

Cut a 6x8" piece of fabric and gather it like an accordion.
Keep the fabric tightly folded in the mat opening and fasten
to the back of the mat. Fan out the fabric at the outside corner and fasten to the back of the mat. The edges of the
opening may be finished using the covered strips of matboard.

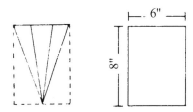

6"

8"

BEVELED MATBOARD "PLAQUES"

This beveled matboard plaque can be used to identify the artist, the title of the art, a date, or any other information about the image in the mat.

MATERIALS:
Two pieces of matboard:
    one piece 4x6" for the plaque
    one piece 6x8" for a support
Pencil and rule
Double-sided tape

1. Apply a small strip of double-sided tape to the back of the 4x6" matboard. Center the 4x6" board on the 6x8" board and press to adhere the tape.

2. Use a pencil and rule to mark the size of the plaque on the face of the matboard, in this case 11/4" x 3 1/2".

3. Place in the mat cutter **face up**, and cut a reverse bevel all the way across the 4x6" board from end to end, following the pencil line. Repeat on the other three sides. The scraps will fall away, leaving the plaque.

4. Remove the plaque from the support board and attach it to the mat with double-sided tape or white glue.

The lettering can be applied to the plaque with rub-on transfer type available at art supply stores.

—or—

Type the information and print it out on a color coordinated paper. Mount it to the matboard using Perfect Mount Film or 3M's PMA before trimming the edges.

Beveled edge matboards can be used to identify work or objects in a frame.

Print out information and attach it to a piece of matboard using Perfect Mount or PMA.

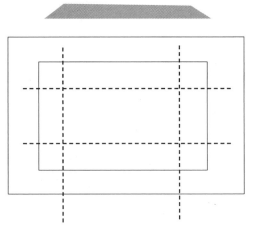

Using a support board will allow for straighter cuts on the open bevel.